Young People's Science Encyclopedia

Ve

Vegetable
Vegetation
Vegetative
  reproduction
Vein
Velocity
Veneer
Venereal disease
Venom
Vent
Venus
Venus's flytrap
Verbena
Vermiculite
Vertebrate
Vertigo
Vesalius, Andreas
Veterinary
  medicine
VHF

Vi

Vibration
Vigneaud, Vincent du
Viking Project
Vinca
Vine
Violet
Virchow, Rudolf
Vireo
Virgo
Virus
Viscera
Viscosity
Vitamin
Vitamin
  deficiency

Vo

Voice
Volcano
Vole
Volt
Volta, Alessandro
Voltmeter
Volume

Volvox
Vomit
Vortex
Vorticella

Vulcanization

Wa

Walking stick
Wallaby
Walnut
Walrus
Walton, Ernest
Warbler
Warburg, Otto
Wasp
Water
Water Bearer
Water buffalo
Watercress
Water
  desalinization
Water lily
Water table
Water vapor
Water vascular
  system
Waterfall
Watershed
Waterspout
Watson, James
Watt
Watt, James
Watt-hour meter
Wave
Waxwing, cedar

We

Weapons
Weasel
Weather
Weather Bureau
Weather
  forecasting
Weather map
Weather station
Weathering
Weed
Weigela
Weight

Weightlessness
Weismann,
  August
Well
Weller, Thomas
Werner, Alfred
West Wind Drift
Westerlies
Wetting agent

Wh

Whale
Wheat
Whelk
Whippoorwill
Whirlpool
White light
White mice
Whitefish
Whitney, Eli
Whooping cough

Wi

Wild flower
Wilderness
Willet
Willow
Wilson, Charles
Wind
Wind sock
Wind tunnel
Wind vane
Windbreak
Windlass
Windmill
Wisteria
Witch hazel

Wo

Woehler,
  Friedrich
Wolf
Wolverine
Wombat
Woodpecker
Wool
Work
Worm
Wound

Wr

Wren
Wright, Orville
  and Wilbur

Xa

Xanthophyll
Xenon
Xerography
X rays
Xylem

Ya

Yak
Yam
Yawn
Yaws

Ye

Yeast
Yellow fever
Yew
Yolk
Ytterbium
Yttrium

Ze

Zebra
Zenith
Zero

Zi

Zinc
Zinnia
Zircon
Zirconium

Zo

Zodiac
Zoo
Zoology
Zygote

YOUNG PEOPLE'S
SCIENCE ENCYCLOPEDIA

Edited by the Staff of
NATIONAL COLLEGE OF EDUCATION, Evanston, Illinois

ASSOCIATE EDITORS

HELEN J. CHALLAND, B.E., M.A., Ph.D.
  Chairman, Division of Natural Sciences
National College of Education,
Evanston, Illinois

DONALD A. BOYER, B.S., M.S., Ph.D.
  Science Education Consultant, Winnetka
Public Schools, Winnetka, Illinois
Science, National College of Education

EDITORIAL CONSULTANTS
ON THE STAFF OF NATIONAL COLLEGE OF EDUCATION

Elizabeth R. Brandt, B.A., M.Ed.
Eugene B. Cantelupe, B.A., M.F.A., Ph.D.
John H. Daugherty, B.S., M.A.
Irwin K. Feinstein, B.S., M.A., Ph.D.
Mary Gallagher, A.B., M.A., Ph.D.
Beatrice S. Garber, A.B., M.S., Ph.D.
Hal S. Galbreath, B.S. Ed., M.S.
Arthur J. Hannah, B.S., M.Ed., Ed.D.

Robert R. Kidder, A.B., M.A., Ph.D.
Jean C. Kraft, B.S., M.A., Ph.D.
Elise P. Lerman, B.A., B.F.A., M.F.A.
Mary M. Lindquist, B.A., M.A., Ph.D.
Mary-Louise Neumann, A.B., B.S.L.S.
Lavon Rasco, B.A., M.A., Ph.D.
Bruce Allen Thale, B.S.Ed., M.S.Ed.
Fred R.Wilkins, Jr., B.A., M.Ed., Ph.D.

SPECIAL SUBJECT AREA CONSULTANTS

Krafft A. Ehricke, B.A.E., H.L.D.
Benjamin M. Hair, A.B., M.D.
Charles B. Johnson, B.S., M.A., M.S.
Raymond J. Johnson, B.B.A., M.Ed.

H. Kenneth Scatliff, M.D.
Eleanor S. Segal, M.D.
Paul P. Sipiera, B.A., M.S.
Ray C. Soliday, B.A., B.S., M.A. (Deceased)

Don Dwiggins, Aviation Editor

THE STAFF

Project Director   Rudolph A. Hastedt
Project Editor   M. Frances Dyra
Senior Editor   Jim Hargrove
Editorial Assistant   Janet Zelasko

Young People's
SCIENCE
Encyclopedia

Edited by the Staff of

NATIONAL COLLEGE OF EDUCATION

Evanston, Illinois

Volume 19/Ve-Zy

 CHILDRENS PRESS ™

CHICAGO

Photographs

Page 2: Skylab space station (NASA)

Page 3: *Top to Bottom:*
Wheatfield (U.S.D.A. Photo)
Technician capping Abbokinase (Abbott Laboratories)
Spider (Macmillan Science Company)
View of Earth (NASA)
Space Shuttle (NASA)
Bahama coral reef (Macmillan Science Company)

Cover: Design by Sandra Gelak
Zebra (Christine Hagel)
Windmill: Holland, Michigan (James P. Rowan)
Spatterdock (James P. Rowan)

Library of Congress Catalog Card Number: 67-17925

Vegetable A vegetable is a plant used as human food. The part of a vegetable that is eaten may come from the stem, the leaf, the fruit, or the root of the plant.

Vegetables are not sweet and, when eaten, are often flavored with salt or spices. They are high in mineral salts and vitamins. Usually, vegetables contain from 70 to 90 percent water. The carbohydrate present is often starch. Except for legumes, the protein content of vegetables is scant. Some vegetables contain slight amounts of fat. One of the most important reasons for including a variety of vegetables in one's diet is for roughage. The *cellulose* content found in vegetables aids the process of digestion and elimination.

Vegetables are often grouped into several categories. *Earth vegetables* develop under the ground as roots, stems, or fleshy leaves. RADISHES, WHITE POTATOES, and ONIONS are examples. *Herb vegetables,* whose parts are grown above the soil as leaves, leaf petioles, and delicate stems, include LETTUCE, CELERY, and ASPARAGUS. *Flower vegetables* are usually picked while the flower is still in bud form. BROCCOLI and CAULIFLOWER are edible flowers. *Fruit vegetables* develop from the ovary and/or the receptacle of the flower. TOMATOES, STRING BEANS, SQUASHES, and OKRA are of this kind. *Seed vegetables* are those from which the fruit wall has been removed. Some seed vegetables are RICE, PEAS, and CORN.

Besides supplying food for man and animals, vegetables are sources of other products. Fixed oil from palms is used in making soap. Wintergreen and peppermint leaves produce valuable volatile oils. Other vegetables have medicinal uses.

Vegetable tans are extracted from various plant tissues, in particular from the bark of oak and chestnut trees. They contain a chemical called *tannin.* Animal hides are soaked in this solution. The tannins combine chemically with the proteins in the hide. This reaction makes the skins more resistant to decay, tougher, more flexible, and more moisture-proof.　　　　　H. J. C.

SEE ALSO: GARDENING, INDIVIDUAL VEGETABLES, VITAMINS

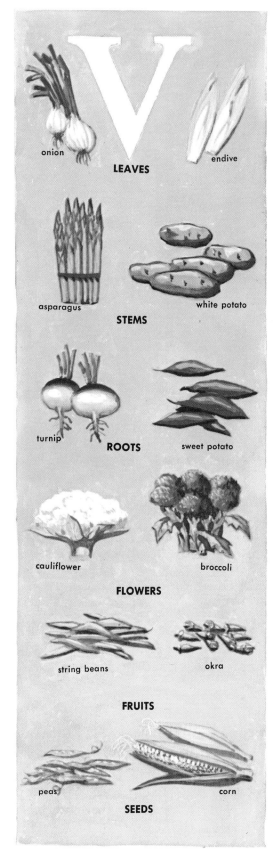

onion　　　　　endive
LEAVES

asparagus　　　　　white potato
STEMS

turnip　　　　　sweet potato
ROOTS

cauliflower　　　　　broccoli
FLOWERS

string beans　　　　　okra
FRUITS

peas　　　　　corn
SEEDS

✳ THINGS TO DO

DO VEGETABLES HAVE FLOWERS?

1 Purchase from the market, or select from your family garden, a variety of vegetables which store food in their roots or stems. Many of these plants are biennials, and, therefore, do not produce flowers until the second year. You will be propagating from the first year's growth.

2 Cut the bottom half off of such roots as a carrot, beet, turnip, radish, and sweet potato. Push the cut ends into a pot of wet sand or vermiculite.

3 Underground stems such as a white potato will root if half of it is submerged in a glass of water. Onion bulbs may be planted directly into a pot of rich garden soil.

4 All of these vegetables will take root, send up new shoots, and soon a flower head will appear.

Vegetation There are four basic types of vegetation, or plant life, on earth —forests, grasslands, tundras, and deserts. The type of vegetation found in an area depends upon such physical factors as climate and soil.

Vegetative reproduction This is any asexual method of producing new plants. Budding, grafting, stem and leaf cuttings, tuberous root, and underground stem propagation are all examples of vegetative reproduction.

Vein The blood vessels which return the BLOOD to the heart are called *veins*. The blood returning to the heart from the body is called *venous* blood, and is dark red in color. However, the blood which is returned through the veins to the heart from the lungs is a bright red because it is rich in oxygen. The blood vessels which can be seen on the back of the hands are veins. Arteries are buried deeper.

Veins begin as very small, thin-walled tubes which increase in size as they near the heart. Blood from the head and arm regions enters the heart through a large vein called the *superior vena cava*. Blood from the trunk and legs is returned to the heart by the *inferior vena cava*.

Medium to large veins are thinner-walled than arteries of the same size but, like arteries, have three coats in their walls. The inside coat is a thin cellular lining (*endothelium*) backed by a thin layer of elastic fibers. As the inner coat grades into the middle coat, the number and thickness of elastic fibers increases and the fibers are encased by smooth muscle fibers. The thickness of the outer coat varies with the size of

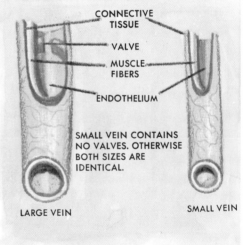

CONNECTIVE TISSUE

VALVE

MUSCLE FIBERS

ENDOTHELIUM

SMALL VEIN CONTAINS NO VALVES. OTHERWISE BOTH SIZES ARE IDENTICAL.

LARGE VEIN   SMALL VEIN

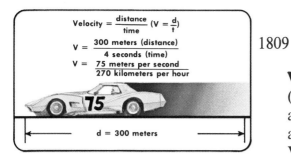

$$Velocity = \frac{distance}{time} \quad (V = \frac{d}{t})$$

$$V = \frac{300 \text{ meters (distance)}}{4 \text{ seconds (time)}}$$

$$V = \frac{75 \text{ meters per second}}{270 \text{ kilometers per hour}}$$

75

d = 300 meters

the vein. Outer connective tissue of the largest veins contains *capillary* networks to nourish vein tissue and a supply of small nerve endings.

Folds in the inner walls of larger veins act as valves to prevent backward flow of blood.   B. J. C.

SEE ALSO: ARTERY, CAPILLARY, CIRCULATORY SYSTEM, HEART, HISTOLOGY

Velocity

Velocity is the speed of an object moving in one direction along a straight line path. Speed is the distance traveled by an object divided by the time it takes the object to move through that distance.

Velocity is the VECTOR quantity used to express the rate of motion of a body. A constant velocity indicates that a body has a constant speed and constant direction.

Units of velocity must contain a length unit, a time unit, and a direction. Twenty kilometers (12.4 miles) per hour, 30° west of north, would be an example.

Speed as used by physicists is a *scalar* quantity; that is, it describes change of position without regard to direction. Newton's LAWS OF MOTION and the related science of MECHANICS study the nature of velocities of bodies. When velocity changes, the moving object shows ACCELERATION or DECELERATION.
          D.A.B.

Vena cava see Circulatory system

Venation see Leaves

Veneer (vuh-NEER) Veneer is a thin layer of a substance usually applied on wood or PLASTIC. It is frequently used on furniture.

Wood veneer is made by slicing a layer as thin as 1/100 inch (.3 millimeter) from a log of beautiful and expensive wood and gluing the layer to the surface of a stronger, but less expensive, wood. Such a method combines strength with texture, and provides an inexpensive desired surface.   D.J.I.

Venereal disease A venereal disease (VD) is passed from one person to another by sexual contact. *Gonorrhea* and SYPHILIS are common types of VD, but the deadliest is AIDS.

SEE ALSO: ACQUIRED IMMUNE DEFICIENCY SYNDROME (AIDS), SYPHILLIS

Venom (VEN-ohm) Venom is a poison liquid that some animals, such as SNAKES, and some arachnids such as scorpions and spiders, secrete and inject into the body by biting or stinging. Snakes produce venom in a type of salivary gland. The venom destroys or impairs the blood corpuscles and lining of blood vessels, or certain nerve centers, or both.

SEE: POISON GLAND, REPTILIA

Vent A vent is the crater-like opening of a VOLCANO from which lava flows. During a volcanic eruption both lava and rock fragments are thrown out of the vent. Vents are commonly found on cinder cone volcanoes, but can also form during flank eruptions.

On larger volcanoes, several vents can occur during a volcano's eruptive lifetime. Each one represents a separate eruption. Generally, after an eruption, the vent fills up with lava and forms a flat, smooth *lava-lake*. In many instances, volcanoes have been known to blow up completely, and the result is that the vent collapses and forms a very wide crater called a *caldera*. The city of Edinburgh, Scotland is built in the caldera of an ancient volcano. Numerous volcanic vents can be seen at Craters of the Moon National Monument in Idaho.   P.P.S.

Ventral Ventral means on or near the abdominal surface of an animal—the front in man and the under side in other animals. Ventral also refers to the surface of a petal that faces the center of the flower.

Ventricle see Heart

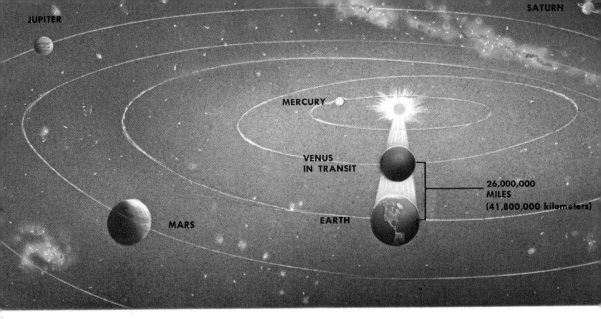

Venus (VEE-nuhs) Venus is the second planet away from the sun. It is almost the same size as Earth. Except for Earth's moon, Venus comes nearer to the Earth than any other heavenly body. There are many mysteries about this planet. A thick blanket of clouds hides its surface.

Venus was named for the Greek goddess of love and beauty. When it is at its nearest point to the Earth, Venus shines like a bright and brilliant star. It is so bright that sometimes it can be seen in daylight. It is more often noticed when it shines like an evening star or a morning star, a few hours after sunset or a few hours before sunrise. Venus is so near the sun that it cannot be seen in the middle of the night, for the same reason that the sun is not seen at night.

Venus's diameter is about 7,700 miles (12,400 kilometers). Its average distance from the sun is 67,200,000 miles (108,000,000 kilometers). Venus's orbit is nearly circular. It completes a revolution around the sun in about 225 Earth days. When Earth and Venus are closest to each other, they are only about 26,000,000 miles (41,800,000 kilometers) apart. This may someday be convenient for space travel.

Venus's orbit is tilted at an angle from the Earth's orbit so that usually Venus seems to be either above or below the sun. On rare occasions Venus crosses the sun, or it goes between the Earth and the sun. These crosses are called *transits.* During transits Venus is seen as a dark disk moving across the sun. These are good times for astronomers to study the planet. Venus crosses the sun twice in about a hundred years. The transists come in pairs, with a period of about eight years between the two transits of the pair. The last transits were in 1872 and 1882. Venus will transit again in 2004 and 2012.

Like the moon and Mercury, Venus goes through phases. Its appearance as seen from Earth changes from crescent to full Venus and back again. Venus seems larger and more brilliant during its crescent stage. Not as much area is seen, but it is nearer to Earth than at full Venus. During its cresent stage, Venus is the brightest object in the sky, except the moon and sun. Venus, when in its full stage, is on the opposite side of the sun from Earth.

Both the United States and Russia have sent spacecraft to study Venus. The United States began the exploration of Venus with the 1962 *Mariner II* fly-by mission. As it passed by the planet, *Mariner II* made observations of the temperature, density, and composition of Venus' atmosphere. In late 1967, the Russians successfully landed a spacecraft on the surface of Venus. Later, Russian landers reported surface temperatures of nearly 750° K. (900° F. or 480° C.) and an atmospheric pressure 90 times greater than Earth's. Upon analyzing the surface material, it was found to be similar to granite.

Because of the very thick atmosphere that surrounds Venus, its surface remains hidden from Earth-based telescopes and

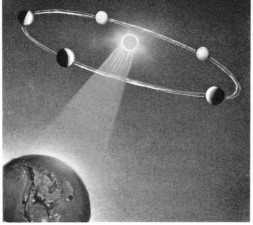

Phases of Venus as seen from Earth are similar to those of the moon. At crescent, Venus is nearest and appears brightest. At "full," Venus is at opposite side of the sun from Earth

Venus's flytrap Venus's flytrap is called an *insectivorous* plant because it eats insects. If an insect lands in the two leaves forming the trap, the leaves snap shut and capture the insect. Certain juices are secreted that digest the animal. The Venus's flytrap does not, however, depend upon insects for food. Since the plant is green it makes food by the process of PHOTOSYNTHESIS. The plant is found along the coast in North and South Carolina.

The Venus's flytrap is a perennial herb of the SUNDEW family. This plant has a rosette of leaves that extend up to 5 inches (12.7 centimeters). From the center of this, a 1 foot (.3 meter) stalk appears with a cluster of white flowers. The petioles on the leaves are expanded at the far end and possess the two-lobed blade or insect trap. The root system is rather poor as is the soil in which it usually grows. The plant uses insects to improve its diet.

The edges of the leaf are fringed with sharp bristles that interlock to hold the insect prisoner. *Enzymes* are secreted by digestive glands located on the upper surface of the leaf. Proteins from the body of the digested insect furnish nitrogen to the plant. In a few days the leaf opens wide, ready to trap another victim, and the parts of the insect's body that are not digestible, dry up and blow away.   P.G.B.

SEE ALSO: PLANTS, INSECTIVOROUS

spacecraft cameras. Several of the Russian landers have survived the intense heat at the surface long enough to transmit pictures back to Earth. These pictures show a surface similar to Earth. Both flat-topped and rounded rocks appear to be common, and suggest an active erosion mechanism at work. Another method of viewing the surface of Venus is by *radar*. Radar easily passes through clouds, and by measuring the signals bouncing back from Venus, scientists are able to reconstruct a picture of the surface. They have found several larger craters, mountain chains, and perhaps the largest volcano in the solar system.

The atmosphere of Venus consists primarily of carbon dioxide, with minor amounts of *sulfuric acid,* water vapor, *hydrofluoric acid,* and perhaps *hydrochloric acid.* This very dense atmosphere is cold in the upper regions and extremely hot at lower levels. This causes a mixing effect that generates high winds and a layering effect based on rising temperatures. Because of these factors, the atmosphere of Venus produces a GREENHOUSE effect, which traps all heat and maintains a constant surface temperature of 750° K. Because the planet rotates on its axis only once every 243 days, the temperatures at the polar regions are the same as at the equator.

It is very unlikely that astronauts will ever walk on Venus, but scientists are learning more about the planet through the use of space probes. In May 1989, the Space Shuttle launched a planetary probe called *Magellan.* After the 15-month journey to Venus, the probe's mission is to make a radar map of the planet's surface.   P.P.S.

SEE ALSO: MOON, PHASES OF; PLANET; SOLAR SYSTEM; SPACE TRAVEL

Venus's flytrap

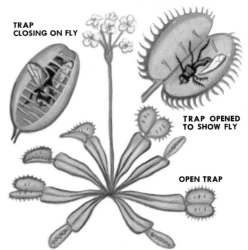

TRAP CLOSING ON FLY

TRAP OPENED TO SHOW FLY

OPEN TRAP

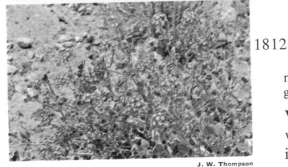
J. W. Thompson

Sand verbena, a variety that requires little water to survive

Verbena (vuhr-BEE-nuh) The verbena family, also called vervain family, includes over 700 kinds of plants. The family, scientific name *Verbenaceae,* includes trees, shrubs and garden flowers.

The common *garden verbena* grows as a perennial in the southern U.S. but as an annual in the north. It is a hybrid which has been developed by crossing wild varieties with cultivated species. Ordinary verbena grows up to a foot (.3 meter) high. The dwarf types rarely exceed 6 inches (15.2 centimeters). The flowers are irregular, with the corolla fused to form two lips. Verbena blooms occur in various colors except yellow. The flower may be one color, striped, or with a different colored center. The leaves are on opposite sides of the stem.

Sand verbena can be found in the Pacific coast area. The trailing stem sends up a flower stalk in the summer. The individual flowers form a pink to lavender ball.

Tuber verbena produces a cluster of purple flowers on a spike. *Moss verbena* is much shorter, with more delicate leaves.   H.J.C.

Vermiculite (ver-MICK-yuh-lyte) Vermiculite is a mineral. It resembles MICA, and may be any one of many different hydrous silicates. It is used as insulation against temperature and sound. It is also used as packing material that is fireproof and in filters used for purifying oil.

Vermiculite does not weigh as much as sand, and is often used as a mulch. It is more easily removed than sand when no longer needed. It is a useful medium in which to start seeds and some cuttings. It is valuable for this purpose because it is sterile and free of weed seeds and insects. Vermiculite has no plant food in it. Minerals must be added if plants are to continue to grow in this potting medium.

Vertebrate Vertebrates have a brain within a skull, a hollow nerve cord, an internal skeletal system of gristle and BONE, and are bilaterally symmetrical. Man is the dominant species of this subphylum of the phylum *Chordata.* SEE: ANIMALS, CLASSIFICATION OF

Vertical take-off and landing see Aircraft

Vertigo (VER-tih-goh) Vertigo is a symptom of a physical disorder or disease of the body. Vertigo is characterized by a sensation of dizziness. Fainting, partial loss of consciousness, loss of equilibrium, or leaning to one side can also be present.

Simple vertigo usually lasts about two weeks, but other cases last until correct diagnosis is made and the cause is correctly treated. Infections, eye trouble, brain injuries, bad teeth, drugs, and seasickness all produce different degrees of vertigo.

The basic cause of vertigo is the disturbance of the three semicircular canals of the inner ear *(labyrinths).* These normally control our balance by means of fluid (which is always parallel to the ground because of gravity), and sensitive nerve receptors, which transmit signals to our brains to report exactly the position of our heads and bodies. Any disturbance of these canals (for example, a virus infection) can make us feel queasy, dizzy, or, in severe cases, unable to stand.   M.R.L./E.S.S.

Vesalius, Andreas (1514-1564) Andreas Vesalius was a Belgian physician who was the founder of modern ANATOMY. He studied medicine at the University of Louvain in Paris.

Upon graduation he was appointed Professor of Surgery and Anatomy at the University of Padua in Italy. Vesalius was a brilliant doctor. He published, at the age of 24, his *Anatomic Tables.* This was followed by *Concerning the Fabric of the Human Body,* the first complete and systematic description of the human body. However, his success and popularity caused great jealousy. Other physicians were already taking credit for some of his work. Deeply hurt by this, Vesalius burned his remaining published notes and ended his teaching career in 1544. He spent the rest of his life as court surgeon to Charles V and Phillip II of France.　D.H.J.

Vesta　see Asteroid

Veterinary medicine

(VET-ehr-in-ary) Doctors of veterinary medicine *(veterinarians)* diagnose, treat, and control injuries and diseases in animals, as well as prescribe and administer vaccines and medicines to maintain healthy animals.

Veterinarians who specialize in the treatment and breeding of cattle, poultry, sheep, swine, and horses are extremely important to food production and public health. They help prevent the outbreak and spread of animal diseases, some of which can be transmitted to human beings. These veterinarians may also inspect meat, poultry, and other foods for public health programs. Some "vets" treat only small animals or pets, and others treat both small and large animals for private interests (zoos, circuses, farms).

In order to become a veterinarian, it is necessary to complete two or three years of college followed by four years at a school of veterinary medicine. Any one who wishes to teach or specialize must have additional training. After this, veterinarians must take and pass a special test to get a license to practice. They can then treat sick animals, prescribe medicines, and perform surgery when necessary.　E.S.S.

SEE ALSO: ANIMAL DISEASES

VHF

VHF refers to *very high frequency* waves. They travel in a very narrow straight path. They are best used in TELEVISION, RADAR, guided missiles, and aircraft RADIO.

SEE: WAVE

Vibration

(vy-BRAY-shun) All substances are made up of very small particles called *molecules.* In some substances, the MOLECULES are close to-

U.S. Department of Agriculture photo

A veterinarian vaccinating a calf against brucellosis, a bacterial infection

gether; in other substances, the molecules are far apart. When the molecules of a substance are sent into motion in WAVES, vibration of the substance occurs.

In materials where the molecules are closer together (for instance, in solids such as steel), the waves travel faster than in substances where the molecules are farther apart (for instance, in liquids such as water.) In LIQUIDS, however, the waves move faster than in air; for in air, which is made up of gases, the molecules are still farther apart. In the air, vibrations strike the ear as SOUND, although the human ear can only hear those vibrations of sound waves in a range from 20 to 20,000 per second. Thus these waves vary in length, though all are extremely short.

An entire mass, such as a *pendulum,* can vibrate, although vibration of an entire mass is generally undesirable. In certain instances, however, vibrating machines are designed for industrial use.　D. A. B.

SEE ALSO: EAR, MUSICAL INSTRUMENTS

Viceroy　see Butterfly

Vicuna　see Llama

Vigneaud, Vincent du

(1901-　) Du Vigneaud was awarded the 1955 NOBEL PRIZE in chemistry for his synthesis of *oxytocin.* Oxytocin is a hormone produced by the pituitary gland in mammals. This hormone is vital to birth and lactation processes.

Du Vigneaud worked on the chemical structure and the physiological importance of INSULIN. During the course of this research, he studied cystine and cysteine.

These two amino acids provide the source for the sulfur found in insulin. This research led to the determination of insulin's structure. Also, he determined the structure of a vitamin called biotin, the synthesis of penicillin, and the synthesis of oxytocin.   A.J.H.

Villi see Digestive System, Pregnancy

Viking Project On July 20, 1976, the first Viking space vehicle landed on the surface of Mars. The second Viking craft landed September 3, 1976. Both spacecraft returned color photos and much scientific data on the conditions on Mars.

The two spacecraft, each weighing nearly 4 tons (3.6 metric tons) had been launched atop giant Titan III/Centaur rockets almost a year earlier. Soon after landing, the *Viking 1* returned amazing color photographs of the Martian landscape. *Viking 2* also returned pictures of its rocky landing site.

Scientists learned many things about Mars' environment. Winds gusted to 40 miles (64 kilometers) per hour and averaged 19 miles (30.5 kilometers) per hour. The temperature at *Viking 1*'s landing site ranged from -122° to -24° F. (-85° to -31.1° C.). Barometric pressures at both sites were between 7 and 8 millibars (Earth's sea level pressure is about 1,000 millibars.). Mars' atmosphere was found to contain 95% carbon dioxide, 2.7% nitrogen, 1.6% argon, and 0.15% oxygen. No evidence of life was found (but then, no proof was found that Martian life does not exist). Examination of thousands of photos from the Vikings revealed a recurring coating of ice frost on the rocks, determined chemically to be water.

One orbiter scored a hairbreadth "near miss" by flying within 17 miles (27 kilometers) of the surface of Deimos, one of Mars' moons. It returned the most

Viking II took many photographs of Mars' surface.

detailed photo of a space object ever taken. It showed surface details as small as a meter (3 feet) across, and threw new light on a theory that Deimos and Phobos, Mars' sister moons, are really captured asteroids.   D.D.

SEE ALSO: ASTRONAUTICS; MARS; SATELLITE, ARTIFICIAL; SOLAR SYSTEM; SPACE VEHICLES

Vinca Vinca, an evergreen plant, is an erect or trailing perennial herb, native to the Mediterranean region, tropical America, India, and Madagascar. Vinca has simple, oval, leathery, shiny green leaves that are opposite each other on the stem. It may have white, pink, or blue flowers.

Vinca minor has small blue flowers. It is commonly called periwinkle, creeping myrtle, or running myrtle. *Vinca major* is widely used in window boxes. It has thin, wiry stems and blue flowers. *Vinca rosea,* commonly known as Madagascar periwinkle, is an erect, everblooming perennial that is very tender. It grows up to 2 feet (.6 meter) tall and has pink or white flowers.   M.R.L.

Vinci see Leonardo da Vinci

Vine Vines are plants that need support in order to grow properly. *Tendrils,* which are bits of stem or leaf, help some vines cling to a structure in order to climb for light. Other vines fasten themselves by sucking cups. Still others entwine themselves about a support. Vines are popular garden plants. They may also grow wild.

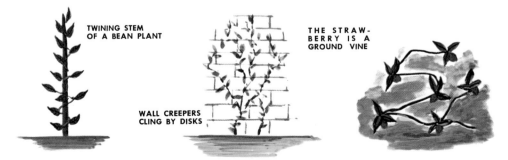

TWINING STEM OF A BEAN PLANT

WALL CREEPERS CLING BY DISKS

THE STRAW-BERRY IS A GROUND VINE

J. W. Thompson

Bird's-foot violet

J. W. Thompson

Desert pansy, an unusual violet

Annual vines grow very quickly. Some perennial vines are raised as annuals in the garden. The MORNING-GLORY is a common annual vine with lovely flowers.

Woody vines with tendrils must have a wall or wire support. They get heavy as they grow old. Some have sucking disks that help them cling to walls. The Virginia creeper and Boston IVY are woody vines.

Creeping, or trailing, vines usually grow along the ground, though English ivy will climb if encouraged. They are useful as ground cover; periwinkle is an example.

Twining vines, or stem climbers, often need a trellis for support. The climbing rose is a twining vine.

Wall, stone, and rock-climbing vines, such as Prairie rose and Dutchman's pipe, require no special support.   M.R.L.

Vinegar see Acetic acid, Acids and bases

Vinyl Vinyl is an inexpensive man-made plastic that is long wearing. It is used to make products, such as records, upholstery, tile, and toys. It comes from ethylene.

Violet The violet is a wild flower or a spring garden flower. There are some 300 species in the Viola family. The PANSY is a cultivated member of this family.

The blue violet grows in shady areas in moist soil. If the plant is in the sun, the heart-shaped leaves will grow very large and attract bumblebees. Perfume, called *viola odorata,* is extracted from the sweet violet

of the garden and greenhouse. The white violet has a yellow center and grows to 12 inches (30.5 centimeters) in height. Johnny-jump-up is in this family.

The violet was a favorite flower of ancient Rome and Egypt; new forms and colors have been produced.

The *African violet* is not a violet. It is closely related to the GLOXINIA.   P.G.B.

Violet ray see Ray, ultraviolet

Viper see Snakes

Virchow, Rudolf (FIHR-kho) (1821-1902) Rudolf Virchow is known as the father of cellular pathology. He stated the basic principles of the formation of blood clots in the blood vessels and proved that cells, not the blood, determined the disease or the health of a body as a whole. He wrote *Cellular Pathology* and *Thrombosis and Embolism.*   D.H.J.

SEE ALSO: PHYSIOLOGY

Vireo Vireo is a small, insect-eating songbird of North America related to the WARBLER. Most have olive or olive-gray plumage.

The vireo

Virgo, the Virgin

Virgo (VER-goh) Virgo is a group of stars that seemed to ancient people to outline the figure of a woman in the sky. Virgo means *Virgin*. In India this group of stars was called the *Maiden*. Virgo can be seen in spring and through the summer. It is east of Leo and south of Boötes. A line of stars makes the Virgin's neck and head. Two curved lines of stars side by side outline her body. Another line of stars stretches out to mark her right arm. The very bright white star on her left side is called *Spica*.

Virgo is the sixth sign of the zodiac. The lines of the celestial equator and the sun's path cross in Virgo. This is the *autumnal equinox*.

One legend says that Virgo represents Astraea, the goddess of justice, who used to live on Earth. When the world grew sinful, Astraea left and took her scales of justice with her. The scales are the constellation LIBRA. The Egyptian legend identifies Virgo with the goddess Isis. One day Isis was frightened by the monster Typhon. As she fled to the sky she dropped a sheaf of corn which scattered through the sky to form the Milky Way. In star drawings, Spica represents some wheat that the Virgin is carrying. C. L. K.

SEE ALSO: BOÖTES, CONSTELLATION, EQUINOX, LEO, ZODIAC

Virilism see Adrenal glands

Virtual image see Lens, man-made

Virus (VY-ruhs) Most viruses are very small (submicroscopic) bodies. They can be seen best only with an *electron microscope*. Viruses will pass through a filter so fine that bacteria, being larger, are strained out.

Usually, when viruses enter a living plant or animal cell, they grow, multiply, and cause disease. Some can live in a cell without harming the victim (host) cell. But if the same viruses enter another kind of host, they produce disease. In addition to causing plant diseases, some viruses cause animal illnesses, as distemper in dogs, and colds, mumps, and influenza in man.

Viruses have various shapes. They may be spherical, rod-like or bottle-shaped. None of them can move by themselves.

Chemically, a virus consists of a core of NUCLEIC ACID, either *RNA, DNA* or both. This core is surrounded by a sheath of non-acid PROTEIN. Some viruses leave the sheath behind when they enter a cell. Others are believed to separate the sheath and acid core right after invading the host cell.

Once inside a living cell, viruses organize the cytoplasmic activities (*enzyme* systems) of the host and start to reproduce. Using raw materials supplied by the host cell, virus particles of RNA or DNA make copies of themselves.

Viruses have been implicated in some types of cancer, leukemia, and Hodgkins disease. To date, there is no solid evidence to prove this. Virus infection, during early pregnancy, may cause deformities in the unborn child. An amazing and frightening achievement was announced in 1967. Doctors Arthur Kornberg and Mehran Goulian at Stanford University in California put together (synthe-

Viruses (arrows) attacking a bacterium (large dark spot) are seen at a 50,000 times magnification, taken by an electron microscope

Photo-micrograph by National Teaching Aids, Inc.

sized) a mixture of chemicals which formed a DNA molecular chain. When this module was absorbed by a bacterial host, the molecules reproduced themselves. A form of life had been made from ordinary, inert chemicals to produce a living, infective virus.

J. C. K.

SEE ALSO: NUCLEOPROTEIN, VACCINE

Viscera Viscera are the organs which lie in the body cavities. They are the heart and lungs in the thorax and the stomach, intestines, spleen, liver, pancreas, and other organs in the abdomen.

Viscosity (viss-KAHS-uh-tee) Viscosity is a measurement which describes the relative ease or difficulty with which a fluid will flow. If one imagines a glass full of a LIQUID to be divided into very small individual layers, viscosity can be understood more easily. It is believed that when a liquid is poured, each layer acts in a manner to resist the flow of the layer above it. The more resistance offered by each layer, the more difficult the flow. Thus, the more *viscous* the liquid, the greater its viscosity.

One of the earliest methods of measuring the viscosity of a fluid was to observe the flow of the fluid through a small tube. A law and a fairly complicated formula were introduced by a scientist named Jean Poiseuille for measuring viscosity. The units of measurement are called *poises* in honor of this man. Although there have been refinements through the years, viscosity can, and still is, measured by the "flow-through-a-tube" method. In addition, however, electrical instruments are now used that contain a revolving spindle immersed in the liquid where viscosity is to be determined. These electric *viscosimeters* read directly in poises, or fractions of poises, called *centipoises* or *millipoises*. Viscosity measurements are very important in quality control of lubricants, in regulating the movement of liquids through pipes, and in analysing blood. M. S.

Vision see Eye, Sense organs

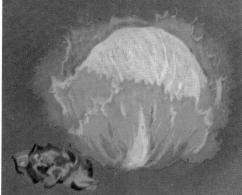
Spinach has more Vitamin A than lettuce.

Vitamin The discovery and study of vitamins began just in the 20th century. As long ago as 1720, it was discovered that citrus fruit juices aided in the treatment of *scurvy,* now known to be a vitamin C deficiency disease. In 1906, an English scientist made the discovery that milk, in addition to being an excellent food, also contains other substances necessary to good health. These substances later became known as *vitamins.*

Then, in 1911, Casimir Funk, a Polish biochemist, found a substance in rice and bran which he used to cure polyneuritis in pigeons. He gave it the name of *vitamine* (Latin: *vita,* life plus *amine,* hydrocarbon). It was soon found that the substance he had discovered was the vitamin B group, also called *B complex.*

The pioneering diet studies by many scientists led to discovering the causes of a number of diseases. The list of vitamins essential to human and other animal life is impressive. They include A, the B's, C, D, K and several known only by their chemical names. Vitamins, then, are definable as organic compounds other than the regular carbohydrates, fats, proteins, and minerals, that are necessary for life processes to continue functioning properly.

Of all vitamins, only A, D, and K can be synthesized by the human body. For example, vitamin A can be built up if *carotene* is included in the diet. Carotene is in carrots, tomatoes, green vegetables, liver and fish oils. Vitamin A aids vision and prevents night-blindness. Vitamin D can be made in our skin when it is exposed to the sun's ultraviolet rays. It can also be obtained from fish-liver oils. In overdoses (in medicines or fortified foods), it can produce adverse physical effects. D enables the body to use calcium and phosphorus to build healthy bones. Vitamin K acts in our blood to help coagulation and reduce bleeding; it is produced by certain bacteria that grow in our intestines.

Of the many vitamins not synthesized in our bodies, C or *ascorbic acid* is the one that aids in formation of tissue-strengthening *collagen.* This keeps cartilage, tendons, and connective tissues healthy, but doses in excess of minimum daily requirements are probably not useful in preventing colds. The body excretes what it cannot use, so a new supply should be taken every day.

The B-complex vitamins are important mainly as *catalysts* (organic ENZYMES) in body METABOLISM. Vitamin B is *niacin* or *nicotinic acid,* present in high-protein foods. It gives resistance to infection. B_1 or *thiamine,* in similar foods, is needed for the body's complete use of carbohydrates. B_2 or *riboflavin* is active in bodily oxidation-reduction, catalyzing the release of energy from foods. The prolonged lack of B_2 causes muscle atrophy in the disease pellagra. B_6 (pyridoxine) promotes the cells' assimilation of proteins for general health. Vitamin B_{12} aids in blood cell replacement and prevents pernicious anemia.   E.Y.K.

SEE ALSO: BLOOD, HISTOLOGY, NUTRITION, PHYSIOLOGY

Vitamin deficiency Vitamin deficiency is the absence in the body of necessary materials ordinarily found in a well-balanced diet. If this deficiency is due to lack of proper foods, it can be corrected by a well-planned diet.

Vitamin deficiencies affect the body by producing fatigue, poor thinking, and nervous reactions. The blood may be affected by *anemia* which produces breathlessness and weakness. The bones may become misshaped and growth stunted.

Before 1911, doctors did not know what caused *scurvy, beriberi, pellagra, rickets,* and other deficiency diseases. In the last sixty years, better education, improved standards of living, and a better understanding of the importance of vitamins have decreased these diseases.

Except in very poor countries, when these diseases are found today, it is generally among people who have badly selected diets, who are addicted to alcohol, or who diet unwisely to reduce. It can be seen from the table (p. 1819) that some vitamins are destroyed by the heat of cooking, so foods should not be overcooked. Other vitamins are dissolved in the water used in cooking. This water can be used in making soups or gravies.

Scurvy was the first recognized vitamin deficiency. Sailors on long ocean voyages often developed scurvy. Lime juice was found to be a curative.

Pellagra is mainly due to a lack of vitamin B_2 (riboflavin) and niacin. This deficiency is common among people living on a diet of corn. The first symptoms are tiredness, lack of appetite, and nervousness. Later, the skin becomes dry and ulcerated. Mental changes may occur, with the person appearing insane. Vitamin B corrects pellagra.

A deficiency of folic acid causes a disease called *sprue,* and the sufferer becomes anemic and develops diarrhea, and the abdomen becomes swollen.

Rickets, a vitamin D deficiency disease, occurs primarily in children who have inadequate diet and little sunshine. This deficiency causes enlarged joints, deformed legs, and distended abdomen. If the disease is untreated in childhood, these bone deformities may be permanent.

There is still much to be learned about vitamin deficiency diseases and the mechanisms affected by vitamins.   J.K.L.

SEE ALSO: MEDICINE, PATHOLOGY, VITAMIN TABLE OPPOSITE PAGE

Viviparous (vye-VIPP-uh-russ) This term refers to animals, usually MAMMALS, that give birth to living young and nourish them when they are yet unborn. In most mammals, the *placenta* brings food and oxygen to the embryos.

SEE ALSO: MAMMALIA

Vixen   see Fox

Vocal cords   see Voice

TABLE OF VITAMINS

VITAMIN	SOURCE	NEEDED FOR	RESULT OF DEFICIENCY
Vitamin A (unsaturated aliphatic alcohol) This substance can be produced in the human system by eating food containing carotene	Carrots, tomatoes, green vegetables, fish-liver oil, liver, egg yolks, cheese	Good vision, resistance to infection, maintenance of epithelial tissue	Nightblindness, dry sore eyes; infection from breakdown of tissue
Vitamin B and B-complex group All water soluble. These are the substances most needed for proper metabolism	Beans, peas, pork, nuts, egg yolk, liver, whole cereals, unpolished rice	Muscular growth, healthy nerves and skin, assimilation of carbohydrates, maintenance of body temperature	Dry, scaly skin; peripheral neuritis; muscular atrophy; beriberi; increased fatigue; emotional disturbances
Vitamin B_c (Folic acid)	Green, leafy vegetables, liver	A curative when used with Vitamin B_{12} for pernicious anemia or when used alone for sprue	Anemia in which red blood cells are larger than normal but few in number (sprue)
Vitamin B_1 (thiamine) This substance cannot be stored in the system and must be constantly replaced. Not destroyed in cooking	Beans, peas, pork, wheat germ, yeast	Complete use of carbohydrates, energy and strength	Fatigue; irritability; loss of appetite; extreme deficiency—beriberi, pellagra, inflamed peripheral nerves, heart changes, weakness, body swelling
Vitamin B_2 or G (riboflavin) Slightly soluble in water. Destroyed by light, not destroyed by heat	Milk, eggs, meats, legumes, green leaves, whole grain cereals, yeast, liver	Bodily energy production as a part of enzyme systems	Inflammation of eyes, skin and nerves; loss of energy; contributes to pellagra
Vitamin B_6 (pyridoxine) and H (biotin)	Liver, eggs, fish, lettuce, yeast, celery, lemon, whole wheat, milk	Assimilation of amino acids and protein for growth and general good health	Weight loss in adults; impaired growth in children; skin lesions; anemia
Niacin (nicotinic acid)	Yeast, chicken, beef liver, tuna fish, halibut, peanuts, lean meat	Healthy tissue, adequate energy	Skin eruptions, weakness, pain, indigestion, diarrhea, great mental disturbances (pellagra)
Vitamin B_{12} (cobalamin)	Meats, especially liver	Production of red blood cells	Pernicious anemia
Vitamin C (ascorbic acid) Soluble in water	Citrus fruits, tomatoes, potatoes, cabbage, spinach	Healthy bones, forming a protein of skin (collagen), tendons, cartilage, connective tissue. Normal functioning of blood vessels, healing, tissue respiration	Scurvy; fragile capillary walls, fracture of bones, bleeding gums, loose teeth, painful joints; slow healing of wounds
Vitamin D This substance can be produced by the human system by exposure of the skin to sunlight. Fat soluble. Normal diets have little if any vitamin D	Limited. Not in natural foods of plant origin. Liver oil, body oils of fish, egg yolk (if hen's diet is high in D)	Body's use of calcium and phosphorus	Rickets; soft bones, bowed legs, defective teeth, enlarging of wrists, knees and ankles (overdoses of D are dangerous)
Vitamin E Soluble in fat	Wheat germ, cotton seed, grain cereals, lettuce, liver, sweet breads (pancreas)	Necessary for good nutrition. Exact role not yet clearly defined.	Repeated miscarriages of pregnancy. Diseases of the nervous system. Certain types of heart disease.
Vitamin K This substance is created in the system by bacteria in the intestinal tract. Fat soluble	Green leaves, soybean oil, egg yolk, liver	Blood clotting	Hemorrhages due to lack of blood clotting

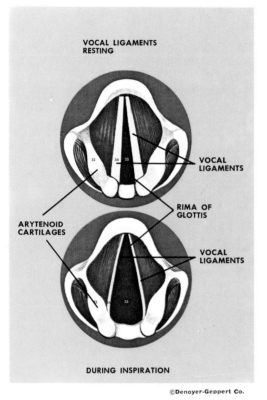

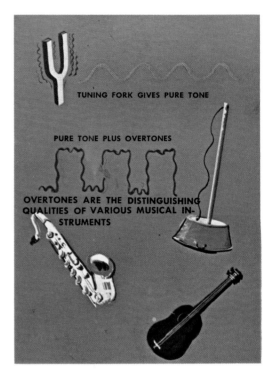

A pure tone is difficult to obtain

Voice Voice is sound made by the vocal organs of people and some animals. Ideas and feelings can be communicated from one being to another by means of the voice. For example, the voice of a chattering robin warns other birds to stay away from the nest. The voice of a barking dog may indicate that a stranger is near. The voice of a crying baby may indicate hunger or sickness. As human babies grow, they learn to use the voice to speak.

No two voices are exactly the same, so the sound of the voice identifies the speaker. Males usually have deeper voices than females. They have longer vocal cords. The singing voice expresses a wider range than the speaking voice. Some voices are uninteresting because they do not vary in tone. This evenness of pitch is known as *monotone*.

QUALITIES OF A GOOD VOICE

Voice depends on volume, pitch, speed, and quality. Voice must be loud enough to be heard; sounds must be distinct; speech must not be too rapid or the sounds will blur together; and speech which is too slow makes the listener become tired and restless. A good voice must not be too highly pitched or it will sound shrill; but when the pitch is too low, the voice sounds rough and harsh. Inflection is the up-and-down movement in pitch and gives the voice melody.

HOW VOICE IS PRODUCED

Voice is produced through the action and interaction of many body parts. Thus the voice often reflects the mental or physical condition of the speaker. Fear, illness, tiredness, excitement, or happiness are easily detected in the sound of the voice.

The *lungs,* the *diaphragm,* the *abdominal muscles,* and the *rib muscles* cause air to move, which is necessary in making sound. The lungs are located in the chest and resemble two elastic, spongy air sacs. The diaphragm is a big muscle located over the stomach and below the lungs. When it contracts air rushes into the lungs. As the dia-

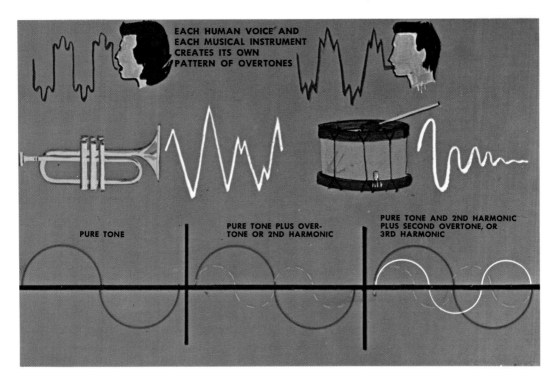

EACH HUMAN VOICE AND EACH MUSICAL INSTRUMENT CREATES ITS OWN PATTERN OF OVERTONES

PURE TONE

PURE TONE PLUS OVERTONE OR 2ND HARMONIC

PURE TONE AND 2ND HARMONIC PLUS SECOND OVERTONE, OR 3RD HARMONIC

Fundamental pitch with harmonic overtones allows a listener to distinguish between voices

phragm relaxes it pushes air out. There are two layers of rib muscles. The outer layer helps the chest expand, and the inner layer helps it contract.

The *trachea,* or windpipe, is like an air hose from mouth to lungs. The *larynx,* or voice box, is at the top of the trachea in the neck. The *vocal cords,* lying across the voice box, enclose two white ligaments. Sound occurs when air passes over the vocal cords, making them vibrate. Tiny, powerful muscles are attached to the vocal cords. These muscles tighten and loosen the vocal cords and thus regulate the pitch and quality of the voice.

Resonators reinforce the quality of sound made by the vocal cords, giving it richness and overtones. The mouth, nasal cavities, and hard palate (roof of the mouth) are resonators. Variations in the size and shape of these resonators are largely responsible for the differences in voices. *Articulators* produce vowels and consonant sounds needed in speech. These sounds are formed by the actions of the lower jaw, lips, teeth, tongue, soft palate, and uvula. The lower jaw controls the size of the mouth opening. The lips focus vocal tones forward in the mouth. Sounds such as *t, th, f,* and *v,* require the

tongue or lips on the teeth to direct sound correctly. The tongue is a flexible mass of muscles. A different sound results from each position of the tongue. The soft palate and uvula form the back wall of the mouth. The uvula is like a valve that can close or open the nasal passage. *K, n,* and *ng* sounds are made at the back of the mouth.

VOICE PROBLEMS

Not all poor voice sounds are caused by bad habits or carelessness of the speaker. Cracked and uncontrolled voices are common among young boys, and are caused by an enlargement of the larynx and vocal cords. Lisping is often caused by missing or deformed teeth. Enlarged ADENOIDS may cause a nasal voice. Nasal voices may also be caused by a cleft-palate, where sound goes into the nasal areas when the roof of the mouth is divided in two sections. Often surgery can correct this condition. The deaf and hard-of-hearing often have speech problems. Voice production is learned by listening to, and imitating, others. If hearing is impaired, it is difficult to learn speech sounds.   M. R. L.

SEE ALSO: OVERTONES, RESONANCE, RESPIRATORY SYSTEM, SOUND

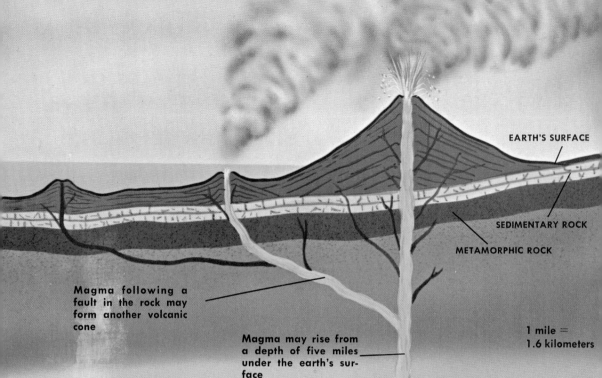

Magma following a fault in the rock may form another volcanic cone

Magma may rise from a depth of five miles under the earth's surface

EARTH'S SURFACE

SEDIMENTARY ROCK

METAMORPHIC ROCK

1 mile = 1.6 kilometers

Volcano (vahl-KAY-noh) Deep under the crust of the earth, a fluid molten material called *magma* is found. This material is in a fluid state because great pressures from above cause very high temperatures. This keeps the magma from cooling into solid rock. When the magma finds its way to the surface through cracks (faults or fissures) in the earth's crust, a volcano may erupt. The magma that reaches the surface is called *lava*.

Often magma will force its way through cracks and breaks in the rock far under the surface. Here it hardens into *igneous rock*, which has large crystalline grains. Igneous rock with small crystals is formed by lava that hardens on the surface.

Volcanoes erupt and flow in different ways, depending on the type of magma. If the content of the magma is more than 60% silica (SiO_2), which has a high melting point, the eruption will often be violent and explosive. Great bubbles of lava are thrown high into the air, cool, and form rocks. The lava, along with ash, dust, and pieces of rock from the earth's crust, rain down on the surrounding area. This type of volcano forms a high steep cone, called a *cinder cone*. It generally does not produce lava from its VENT, but from flank eruptions.

When a volcano has low silica-content lava associated with it, the eruption may start with a rising column of smoke in a level area, with ash and lava flowing out. There is very little explosive action. Sometimes the lava will find an opening many yards away from the original eruption. This type of volcano builds up a rim more slowly, with more gradually sloping sides. Escaping lava will travel in very fast rivers. The rock will cool and harden on top of the river of lava, break off in blocks, and be carried along on the hot molten stream underneath. There may be holes (*fumaroles*) near volcanos that release streams of smoke.

Volcanos form in particular geographical areas. One volcano, called the *shield* or Hawaiian Island-type, forms in oceanic regions or along the margins of the ocean. These volcanos generally have a low-silica lava and are not considered to be very explosive. This type of eruption forms rock called BASALT. The second volcano type is called *continental*, because it primarily occurs on the continental land masses. This volcano produces high- silica lava, and as it cools forms *rhyolite*. A third type of volcano, called a *composite*, can occur along the margins between the distinctly oceanic and continental regions. In one manner or another, all volcanos are related to PLATE TECTONICS.

Volcanos sometimes cause great damage, and create many changes on the surface of

✳ **THINGS TO DO**

WHAT IS INSIDE A VOLCANIC MOUNTAIN?

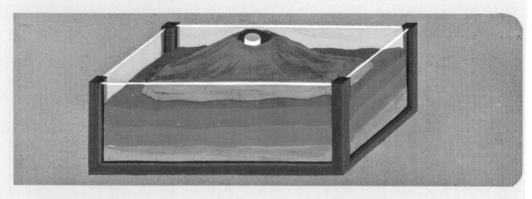

1   Purchase several packages of different-colored modeling clay. Let each color represent a kind of rock: the lower layer will be igneous; the second layer will be metamorphic; the top layer will be sedimentary.

2   Construct a wood and glass frame for the cut-away of a volcano. Groove the wooden ends and base in order to slip in the glass sides. Leave one side open until the layers are modeled. Follow the illustration for details. Slip on the other glass side when completed.

3   Build up a volcanic cone on top, leaving a hole or crater. Insert a small metal can in the crater. Fill the can with fine ammonium dichromate crystals (from a drug store). When this is ignited, it burns, forming a dark green ash which tumbles over the cone in the same manner as lava flows in a real volcano, gradually building up into a mountain.

the earth. An extinct volcano can become a lake, like Crater Lake in Oregon. When the pool of lava in the center cools and slowly sinks into the earth, water collects and a lake is formed. The rim and slope also may be slowly worn away by EROSION, leaving a hardened neck of lava such as forms the Devil's Tower in Wyoming.   V.V.N./P.P.S.

SEE ALSO: EARTH, GEOLOGY; INTRUSION; PAHOE-HOE LAVA

Vole   Vole, or field mouse, is a burrowing, plant-eating rodent of the rat family. It has a short, hairy tail, a blunt nose, and rootless molar teeth. It is larger than a house mouse.

SEE: RODENTIA

Meadow vole

Volt One volt is the amount of electrical potential difference across a conductor having a resistance of one OHM that makes a current of one AMPERE flow in the conductor. Ohm's law relates the three units: volt, ampere, and ohm.

The common flashlight cell has 1½ volts. Commercial electricity enters one's house at either 110 or 220 volts.

Electromotive force (emf) is the pressure of electrons. Voltage is a measure of this electron pressure somewhat the same way pounds per square inch or grams per square centimeter is a measure of water-pipe pressure.

A battery consists of two or more cells, connected in series; and each cell adds its voltage to the rest. Thus the common six-volt lantern battery has four, one and one-half volt dry cells. An automobile battery is made of cells of another type, the lead-sulfuric acid cell, each unit of which gives

2.0 volts. Since a car's starter motor, lamps, and spark-coil system are designed to work on twelve volts, a car battery has six such two-volt cells connected in series. Parallel-connected batteries do not increase the voltage. They are used where larger currents are needed.

The alternating current commonly used in American homes, offices, and factories comes along transmission lines from generator stations. In these lines, electric current is moved at very high voltages because less heating loss is produced in the wire this way. Long-distance lines often employ over 100,000 volts. At points along the way, the voltage is stepped down by transformers to the 110 or 220 volts used in homes and offices.

Voltages in radios may range from 150 to 1500 volts. In television sets, voltages of 20,000 volts exist at certain points. These voltages are obtained by stepping up the household voltage of 110 volts, using transformers.

Lightning and experimental machines can generate voltages of more than one million volts.   D. A. B.

SEE ALSO: ELECTRICITY, NUCLEAR ENERGY, TRANSFORMER

Volta, Alessandro (1745-1827) Volta was an Italian physicist who was a pioneer in electrical discovery. He invented the *electrophorus,* an apparatus used in generating static electricity, and the *electroscope,* which could detect small charges of electricity and tell whether a charge was positive or negative. He also invented an electrostatic pistol and the electrical CONDENSER, but he is especially known for inventing the first true battery.

It was in 1800 that Volta developed the battery, or voltaic pile. He found that by placing metal disks of zinc and copper alternately in a pile and separating them by pieces of cloth wet with acid or salt solution, a useful source of electricity is created. Because of this great achievement in electricity the name *volt* (from Volta) came into use as one of the units in this field.

Volta's work was appreciated almost immediately, not only by his fellow scien-

Alessandro Volta

tists, but also by the political heads of state. In 1801 Napoleon called him to Paris, and a special gold medal was given him. He also was made a senator in Italy and given the title of "count." Volta returned to Como in 1819, and on March 5, 1827, died there in the city of his birth.   M. S.

SEE ALSO: BATTERY, ELECTRICITY, VOLT

Voltmeter A voltmeter is an instrument used to measure the voltage or difference in electrical pressure between two points of an electrical circuit. The meter is placed across that part of the circuit where the voltage is to be measured.

Because direct current (DC) circuits have a steady voltage and alternating current circuits (AC) have a varying, pulsating voltage, voltmeter construction must be designed to allow for these differences.

Direct currents are usually measured by a *moving-coil,* permanent magnet voltmeter or by a *fixed-coil,* moving magnet meter. The moving-coil meters use the most common of electric meter designs, the *D'Arsonval* movement. The current from the external circuit flows through the moving coil of the meter and sets up a magnetic field around the coil. This field opposes the field due to the permanent magnet, and the coil is made to rotate. The coil rotates until the force of the opposing magnetic fields is just balanced by the mechanical force of the springs on which the coil is suspended. The larger the current, the greater the rotation of the coil. Since a pointer is attached to the movable coil, as the coil rotates the pointer indicates

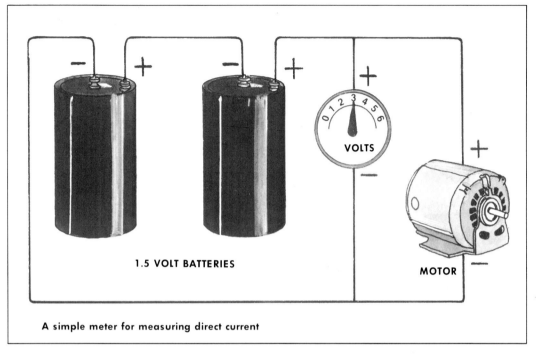

1.5 VOLT BATTERIES

VOLTS

MOTOR

A simple meter for measuring direct current

the voltage-value on a scale calibrated (marked off) in volts.

Fixed-coil, moving magnet voltmeters are, in principle, similar to moving coil meters except that it is the permanent magnet that rotates with the pointer attached. A fixed coil surrounds the magnet.

Alternating voltages are measured with moving-vane meters, THERMOCOUPLE meters, copper oxide rectifier meters, vacuum tube voltmeters, or solid state voltmeters.

In the *moving-vane* meter, a moving vane of soft iron is pivoted within a circular coil. When current flows through the coil, the moving vane is attracted by the field of the coil. As the vane moves, the pointer attached to the vane moves across a scale.

In the solid state voltmeter, diodes are used to rectify AC current. Solid state voltmeters are multimeters capable of reading volts and ohms. These meters perform all the functions of vacuum tube meters but do so with better accuracy.

In a *vacuum tube* voltmeter, a vacuum tube isolates the input circuit of the meter from the circuit being measured. The AC is sometimes rectified by the tube and the resultant DC is fed to a D'Arsonval meter. At other times, the AC is merely amplified and fed directly to an AC meter.   E.I.D.

SEE ALSO: ELECTRICITY, VOLT

Volume Volume is the space occupied by a body. The method of measuring volume depends upon the shape of the body. Volume of a rectangular solid is found by multiplying the length by the width by the depth. MEASURE-MENT is always in cubic units.

Voluntary muscles see Muscle tissue

Volvox (VALL-vohx) A volvox is a green organism (living animal-like plant) shaped like a round ball and only 1/50 inch (.5 millimeter) wide. It lives in ponds of fresh water. This tiny organism is really made up of numerous cells arranged in a hollow sphere. Each cell has two long whips, called *flagella.* As these beat, the volvox rolls through the water.

The volvox belongs to a large group of one-celled organisms that have bodies made of only one cell. Since the volvox is made of numerous tiny cells, it is really a *colony.*

The individual members of the colony work together. If, for example, each cell tried to move in a different direction, the

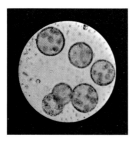

Volvox shows as a hollow ball of hundreds of cells. It is a colony. This example has daughter colonies inside it

Photo-micrograph by
National Teaching Aids, Inc.

ball would get nowhere. However, the flagella beat in such a way that the same end always moves forward. Thus, this round organism has a front and back end. Also, the cells in the rear are specialized for reproduction.

The volvox is called a plant-animal. Like animals, it moves from place to place and moves with lashing flagella. Like plants, it has chlorophyll and carries on PHOTOSYN-THESIS. The cells also have rigid cellulose walls, like those usually found in plants.

E. P. L.

SEE ALSO: PROTOZOA

Vomit Vomiting occurs when the contents of the stomach are thrown up through the mouth. It may be a symptom of disease or it may mean only that the person ate something which cannot be digested.

Vomiting occurs when the abdominal muscles and the muscular walls of the stomach contract suddenly or spasm. These contractions, called *retching,* which eject the stomach's contents, are caused when the membrane of the stomach is irritated by disease, by overloading the stomach, or by eating spoiled or bad-tasting food. Nervous reactions, sickness, odors or sights, or drugs which stimulate the vomiting center of the brain may also cause vomiting.   M. R. L.

Von Baer see Baer, Karl Ernst von

Von Braun see Braun, Wernher von

Vortex A vortex is a mass of whirling fluid which spirals in toward its center. A *whirlpool* is a vortex. It tends to form a VACUUM in the center which draws objects into it.

Vortex

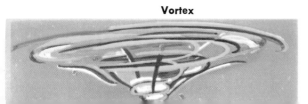

Vorticella

Vorticella (vawr-tuh-SELL-uh) Vorticella is a form of protozoan with a bell-shaped body at the end of a stalk. It is found abundantly in fresh water ponds and lakes. It looks very much like little up-side-down bells on a stalk.

Vorticella is protozoan, characterized by cilia, or fine hairs. In Vorticella the cilia grow along the edge of the bell. They cause a vortex of water to form, bringing into the mouth food which consists primarily of bacteria. In case of danger the edge on which the cilia are located can be folded to cover the mouth.

Often Vorticella lives in colonies. Sometimes it attaches to pond plants, tadpoles, snails, or turtles.   D. J. I.

SEE ALSO: PROTOZOA

VTOL (Vertical take-off and landing) see Aircraft

Vulcanization (Vuhl-kuhn-uh-ZAY-shun) Raw RUBBER is sticky and plastic. It hardens in cold and softens in heat, and it is not elastic. In 1839, Charles Goodyear discovered that by combining raw rubber with sulfur and heating it, the rubber became stronger, elastic, unaffected by heat and cold, and resistant to solvents. Today almost all rubber, as well as synthetic rubber, is vulcanized. The degree of hardness varies directly with the amount of sulfur and heat used in the process.

Vulture see Birds of Prey

Walking stick

Walleyed pike

A wallaby is a kangaroo

Walking stick The walking stick is an insect that looks like a twig without leaves. Its body is thin and its three pairs of legs are long and awkward. The walking stick in the United States has no wings. It is a tree insect with a greenish-gray or brown color that makes it look like a twig when it is not moving. The shape and color of the walking stick help protect it from its enemies. This kind of color is called *protective coloration.*

The walking stick moves so slowly that it hardly seems alive. It walks among the branches of trees and lies in the sun with its long antennae-legs stretched out in front. It is a greedy leaf-eater and may sometimes harm trees. The female drops the shot-like eggs to the ground, where they lie neglected through the winter or even longer. The young walking sticks molt (lose their skin) five or six times, but otherwise are similar to adults.

Because the walking stick cannot bite, sting, or move quickly, it depends on its ability to look like a stick to escape its enemies. Some walking sticks have bark-like markings and even feel like a twig. If a walking stick is caught by a leg, it can break the leg off and escape. This form of protection by means of self-amputation is called *autotomy.*   H. J. C.

SEE ALSO: AUTOTOMY, INSECTA, PROTECTIVE COLORATION, REGENERATION

Wallaby (WAHL-uh-bee) Wallabies, like their big brothers, the kangaroos,

are pouched MAMMALS. They are native to Australia. Wallabies are usually gray or brownish, and they move rapidly on long hind feet. Their long, flat tails are used for balancing. There are twenty-eight kinds of wallabies. They range from rabbit size up to the size of a small kangaroo.

Most wallabies feed at night on grass and leaves. Their speed and dodging ability make them very hard to see or catch. Thus, they are protected from their enemies—the dingo, rock python, eagle, and man. Some species of wallabies form colonies; others live alone. Most of them live on plains and nest in small natural depressions in the ground.

Like other MARSUPIALS, the young (usually one) are born immature. They crawl along their mother's fur to reach her pouch. They attach themselves to their mother's nipple and stay there until they have finished their development.

The *wallaroo,* also a kind of kangaroo, is larger than the wallaby.   J. C. K.

SEE ALSO: KANGAROO, MARSUPIAL

Wallace, Alfred Russel see Darwin, Charles Robert

Walleyed pike see Perch

Black walnut tree, fruit and leaves

Walruses live in the Arctic seas.

Walnut Walnut trees have long, compound leaves and delicious tasting nuts. *Black walnuts* have hard, thick shells. *English walnuts* have thin shells.

The dark brown nuts of the black walnut are wrapped in a tough, green husk early in the fall. When the husk comes off, a brown dye may stain hands. The leaves and nuts have a strong aroma. The hard, lovely grained wood is used for furniture and gunstocks. It is becoming rare.

English walnuts were introduced in the United States from Europe. These delicately flavored nuts are widely grown in California.

Smaller than the black walnut, the *white walnut* or *butternut,* with soft, whitish wood, grows in eastern states. C. L. K.

Walrus The walrus is a mammal of the Arctic seas. These marine mammals have small eyes and nostrils, a stubby and broad snout, coarse, spike-like whiskers, no ears on the outside, and two teeth that form long, yellow-white tusks. These canine teeth grow to be 15 to 30 inches (38 to 76 centimeters) long and weigh up to 9 pounds (4 kilograms). They are used for getting food and defense.

Males can be 12 feet (3.7 meters) long and have an average weight of 2,500 pounds (1,134 kilograms). The female is slightly smaller. Swimming in cold waters of the north, the warm-blooded walrus needs its thick, wrinkled skin covering from ½ to 3 inches (1.3 to 7.6 centimeters) of blubber.

Its feet are modified into flippers. The hair is very sparse and the color is the same in both sexes. Walruses feed upon certain mollusks, crustaceans, and worms.

There are two kinds of walruses, the *Atlantic* and *Pacific walruses,* the latter having longer tusks and shorter whiskers. During the Ice Age, the ice moving south forced animals ahead of it. Consequently, walrus fossils have been found halfway down the Atlantic coast in the United States.

The polar bear, killer whale, and human hunters are the chief enemies of the walrus. The hide is used for leather, the flesh for meat and valuable oil, and the ivory tusks for weapons and ornaments.

Walruses migrate down to the Bering Sea in the fall and return to the Arctic Ocean in the spring. The female has one pup, which spends much time riding piggy-back. It needs to nurse until its canines (tusks) are long enough to scoop up its own food. This may take two years. H.J.C.

SEE ALSO: MAMMALIA, SEAL.

Wapiti see Deer family

Walton, Ernest Thomas S. (1903-   ) Ernest Walton shared the 1951 NOBEL PRIZE in physics with JOHN COCKCROFT. Together they made an accelerator for studying subatomic particles.

With one of the first particle accelerators, these scientists were able to produce very high voltages by using a voltage multiplier. This enabled them to produce very fast subatomic particles. They were able to bombard lithium nuclei with hydrogen ions to produce helium nuclei. A.J.H.

Warbler Warblers are small, active American birds. They are often called the "jewels of the forest" because of their many brilliant colors. Warblers are among the best-loved birds in America. An American warbler called the *oven bird* is so-named because of the oven-like nest it builds.

Warblers eat insects and may be found darting in and out of the leaves of trees looking for food. They are very quick and can easily catch a fly while it is in flight. Warblers do not warble, but have a high-pitched, lisping call. They are called warblers because they resemble the European warblers which belong to a different family.

Warblers spend the winters in the tropical or subtropical south. Many live there all year round, but others migrate to the northern United States and Canada. During their migration in the spring and fall, they may be found all over the United States. Over 150 species of warblers are known, but only half of them migrate.   M.R.L.

SEE ALSO: MIGRATION

Warburg, Otto H. (1883-1970) Warburg was a German biochemist who received the 1931 NOBEL PRIZE in physiology and medicine.

Dr. Warburg's scientific interests were concentrated around three fundamental biological problems: cellular respiration, photosynthesis, and cancer. He researched and identified enzymes as members of the respiratory chain. His investigations into the metabolism of cancer cells led him to believe that cancer cells are capable of growth without oxygen.   P.P.S.

Warm front see Weather forecasting

Wart A wart is a small, tumorous growth on the skin, possibly caused by a VIRUS. Warts can be removed by excision or cauterization (by heat, or chemicals, or X-ray).

SEE: BIRTHMARK, MOLE

Wart hog see Pig

Courtesy Society For Visual Education, Inc.
Paper wasp

Wasp A wasp is a winged insect. The female wasp has a very strong, poisonous sting. The males do not sting. Most wasps live in societies or colonies. They are known as *social* insects. A few species live alone, with each female making its own nest and caring for the eggs.

Wasp is the name given to several species of stinging insects of the order *Hymenoptera*. The wasp, sometimes called a *hornet,* has a slender body with the abdomen attached to the thorax by a slender waist. One familiar wasp is yellow and black, and resembles bees in many ways. The colonies include males, females, and workers. Like BEES, wasps have a queen. The queen lays an egg in each cell of the nest.

The nest of the wasp is built in a tree, in a wall, or on the ground. The nest is made of chewed wood pulp, a paper-like material that is made by the wasps. The nest is built in layers of six-sided cells that form the comb. These cells are then arranged in tiers, and there may be as many as forty layers, or tiers, in a single nest. The only opening into the nest is a small place that allows the wasps to enter and leave. Wasps always work backward when they are building their nests so they will not walk on the moist, newly-constructed cells. As they work, they test the thickness of the cell walls with their feet. The young wasps are cared for in the cells of the comb.

In the fall, all of the wasps die with the exception of a few females. These females spend the winter under rocks or in other hidden places. Old nests are never re-used. Wasps eat sugar, fruit, and honey. They may sometimes eat meat.   M. R. L.

SEE ALSO: INSECTA

The earth's surface distribution of water and land area can be plotted. From 60° N. Lat. to 60° S. Lat. and from 0° Long. to 120° Long. amounts to a total of 30% dry surface

CAN YOU MAKE WATER BOIL BY COOLING IT?

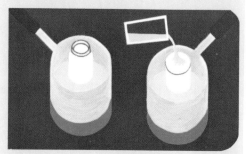

1 **Put an inch of water into a pyrex bottle. Place the bottle in a pan of water on the stove. Heat until the water in the bottle has boiled at least five minutes.** 1 inch = 2.5 centimeters
2 **Turn off, or remove the source of heat. The water will stop boiling. Immediately cap the bottle and turn it upside down in the pan of water.**
3 **Slowly pour a glass of ice water over the bottle. Does the water start to boil again? Why? In discovering the answer to this problem, consider the difference in air pressure.**

Water Without water, there could be no life. The bodies of plants and animals contain more water than any other substance. Water plays a bigger part in man's daily life than anything else except the air he breathes. Yet water is so plentiful that man seldom thinks about it. In addition to water for personal use, man also uses water for power and transportation.

Water covers about 70 per cent of the earth's surface. By its movement, it alters the face of the earth. Water currents help determine climate: without the GULF STREAM, for instance, Great Britain and northern Europe would be so cold that it would be difficult for man to live there. Because water runs downhill, it creates a force which can be harnessed as electric power to drive the machines of factories and homes. Its SURFACE TENSION enables rain to fall in small drops. It provides a means for inexpensive transportation of man and materials to almost any place on earth. It acts as the universal solvent because it dissolves so many different compounds. Bromine used in antiknock gasoline is produced from SEA WATER; potash for fertilizer, from inland waters.

When converted to steam, water expands about 1700 times, creating a power that can drive a locomotive. Because water is almost incompressible, it is used for many engineering tasks. Though it is a poor conductor of heat and electricity, it has a higher specific heat than most substances. It has been adopted as the standard for measurements of specific gravity and specific heat.

Water makes up the greater part of protoplasm, the fundamental substance of life. The blood of man and the sap of plants are primarily water. Plants could not manufacture starch without water. Of course man must drink a great deal of water: if he did not drink water for eight or ten days, he would die. Man's body, in fact, is more than two-thirds water.

Pure water has the chemical formula of H_2O (two parts hydrogen and one part oxygen in every molecule). It is a liquid in its natural state. Pure water does not exist absolutely in Nature. Even rainwater has microscopic particles of dust in it. Seawater is *saline,* that is, it contains a great deal of mineral salts, such as *sodium chloride.* Seawater also contains small amounts of other elements, such as gold. Springs and deep wells often contain relatively large amounts of such minerals as *calcium carbonate.*

Since water is the fundamental substance of human life, health centers have been established to test water and to study and recommend means to eliminate harmful impurities in water that will be used for human consumption. In highly populated areas, where water is taken from rivers or lakes, the city operates a PURIFICATION plant, designed and established by engineers trained in this work.

There are many water-purification methods, the most practical one being the addition of CHLORINE to the water. Water in swimming pools is also rendered safe by the use of chlorination to prevent contamination.

The term *hard water* generally refers to water containing large amounts of calcium and magnesium chlorides and sulfates. When these minerals are absent the water is considered *soft*. Calcium carbonate is also found in water, and it is this salt which appears on the bottom of a teakettle after a period of time as a white, scaly substance. There are several ways of softening hard water; the most popular method now used is the *cation-exchange* process. This method exchanges the magnesium and calcium cations for sodium and potassium. This exchange occurs because the sodium and potassium salts of chlorides and sulfates are very soluble, and will keep the salts from coming out of the water in the form of a precipitate (which would cause the water to become hazy.) There is another process called *deionization* which removes salts from solution through the use of certain resins.   M. S.

SEE ALSO: CURRENTS, OCEAN; ION; LIQUID; MAGNESIUM; SALT; SODIUM

Water, heavy   see Heavy water

Water Bearer   About 28,000 years ago, the zodiac was invented to mark the yearly path of the sun and the major planets. The zodiac was divided into 12 divisions of 30 degrees each. *Aquarius,* which is the Latin word for "water bearer," was made the eleventh sign in the ZODIAC. This large constellation was thought to outline a man pouring water out of a jar into the mouth of a fish which is known as Pisces Australis.

Aquarius, the Water Bearer

The CONSTELLATION was given the name Aquarius by the ancients because the sun is in this sign during parts of January and February, the rainy season in Italy and Egypt. The Egyptians even thought that the floods of the Nile were caused by this constellation. The symbol for Aquarius represents running water.

Aquarius contains no bright stars and is not conspicuous. In late July, it rises at sunset due east and continues in the evening sky until late January. In late September, it appears on the meridian about ten o'clock.

     D. A. B.

Water beetle   see Beetle

Water buffalo   The water buffalo is a member of the ox family. It lives in the swamps and marshes of India, the Philippines, and Africa, and spends much of its time standing shoulder high in the water or wallowing in the mud.

The water buffalo of India is often 5 feet (1.8 meters) high, and very strong. Tame ones are important to the farmers of India, for they not only pull plows and do other heavy farm work, but can work easily in deep mud and in the watery rice fields.

Other water buffaloes are the Cape and Congo buffaloes of Africa, and the smaller carabao and tamarau of the Philippines.

Carabao, a Philippine water buffalo

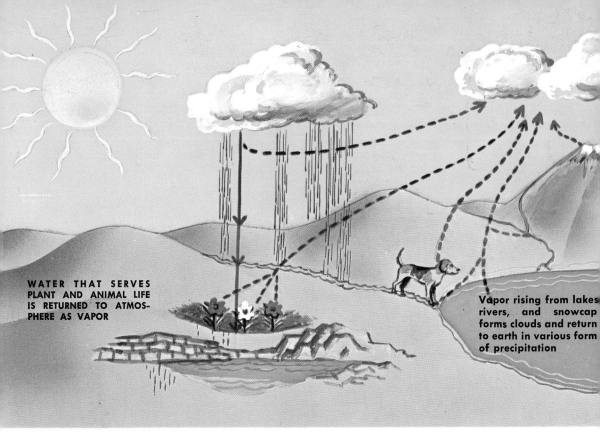

WATER THAT SERVES PLANT AND ANIMAL LIFE IS RETURNED TO ATMOSPHERE AS VAPOR

Vapor rising from lakes rivers, and snowcap forms clouds and return to earth in various form of precipitation

The female water buffalo gives a large amount of milk that is nourishing but has an odd flavor. Both males and females have large horns that curve back, and a tough bluish-black hide.　　　　J. M. C.

SEE ALSO: OXEN

Water bug see Bugs

Watercress　Watercress is a low, trailing HERB. Its leaves and stems are often found floating in shallow waters. Leaves and stems of watercress are used as a garnish and in salads. The leaves must be picked before the flower buds develop or they are too bitter to eat.

This perennial plant has tiny white flowers. Seeds are usually planted in moist soil. The seedlings are transplanted and raised in greenhouses in running water. *Swedish cress,* also called *upland* cress or *winter* cress, is bitter and should be cooked in several waters. The cresses are rich in minerals. Water cress resembles the water hemlock, a poisonous herb.　　　P. G. B.

Water cress

Water cycle The water cycle, also called the *hydrologic cycle,* is the round-trip story of a raindrop. It involves all the water of the earth. Without the water cycle, there would be no rain, and life could not exist to the extent it does now.

The water cycle begins with *evaporation* on the water surfaces of the earth—the oceans, lakes, rivers, and even small pools of water that form during a rain. The heat of the sun slowly turns some of the water into a gas called *water vapor*. This water vapor is carried up into the atmosphere by wind currents.

Because warm air is lighter than cold air, the warm, moist air is pushed upward. As these warm air masses rise high above the earth, they are cooled. When the water vapor is sufficiently cooled, it starts to condense.

In order to condense, water vapor must form around a microscopic piece of dust. This dust is then called a *condensation nucleus.* As condensation occurs, clouds are formed. The tiny drops of water that make up a cloud are light enough to be held up by the air. If the cloud is further cooled, the tiny water droplets combine and fall as rain. If the water droplets are cooled to a low enough temperature, they will fall as snow.

On the surface, raindrops may become a part of little streams or mighty rivers. Not all of the water will reach the sea. Some will immediately become water vapor and again begin the water cycle. Some of the rain will be soaked into the ground and retained in the capillary pores of the soil for plant use. Another part will drain slowly into underground waterways or rock crevices. Much later, this water will again reach a lake, sea, or pond where it evaporates once more.

H. S. G.

SEE ALSO: CONDENSATION, EVAPORATION, PRECIPITATION, WEATHER, WIND

Water desalinization Water desalinization is the process by which salt water is changed to fresh water. Sea water covers nearly 78% of the earth's surface, but this water cannot be consumed because of its high mineral content.

Water suitable for human use should not exceed a few thousand parts per million(ppm) of salt content. Sea water contains about 35,000 ppm of dissolved minerals. Today water suitable for drinking and irrigation can be produced from sea water by several methods. When sea water is boiled, the steam that is produced consists of fresh water. When the steam again has condensed into liquid, it is safe to drink. This is a widely used technique, but it is too expensive to be practical on a large scale. Freezing has a similar effect in that the resulting ice is also fresh water.

Electrodialysis is another method of desalinization. In this procedure electrical current is used to force the salt ions in the sea water to be attracted to electrodes until only fresh water that remains. This process, too, is costly. At the present there is no inexpensive way for desalinization of sea water.

P.P.S.

SEE ALSO: OCEANS

Water flea see Daphnia

Water lily The water lily is a plant. Its fleshy tuber, or *woodstock,* is buried in mud. The large, shield-like leaves grow under the water or float. A single flower is usually raised above the water.

Some species bloom in the day and close their flowers at night; others bloom at night and close their blossoms in the day. The flowers vary in color, though the white water lily is most common.

The water lily grows in both temperate and tropical zones. The white, fragrant *Nymphaea adorata* is common in eastern North America. The yellow *Nuphar advenum* is common to the eastern States and Canada. *Victoria regia,* the giant water lily of the Amazon, has leaves 6 feet (1.8 meters) in diameter and flowers 18 inches (45.7 centimeters) across. The lotus of Egypt, India, and China comes under the general classification of water lily. J.C.K.

Water moccasin see Snakes

Water power see Dam, Energy, Hydroelectric power

Water table When rain falls, some of the water soaks into the ground. Plants use some of it, but much of the water sinks deeper into the soil. Gravity draws it through rocks that contain small holes or cracks. As it seeps through this porous rock, the water continues on until it reaches a level of total *saturation.* That level is called a water table. Water is held in the space because a solid, or *impermeable* rock lies beneath it. Capillary action helps to retain this level.

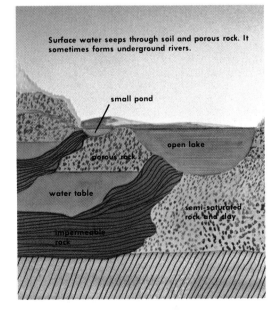

Surface water seeps through soil and porous rock. It sometimes forms underground rivers.

small pond

open lake

porous rock

water table

semi-saturated rock and clay

impermeable rock

The lower limit of the water table is a rocky base. This rock base which holds the water in place may be quite uneven, but it lies generally in the same plane as the land surface above it. It is not flat like a table top.

The water table level is of great importance to farmers, or to anyone who drills a well for water supply. It varies during each season according to the amount of rainfall and to the requirements of plants during the growing season. It is usually lower at the end of the summer season, and rises during the spring and winter because of reduced plant demands.   D. E. Z.

SEE ALSO: WELL

Water vapor Water vapor is the vaporized, or gaseous, form of water. It is invisible. There is water vapor everywhere—in the outside air, inside houses and buildings.

Water evaporates constantly from oceans, lakes, rivers, and from the grassy portions of the earth. As water is heated, the molecules move faster and faster until they bounce out into the air, independently of each other.

Water vapor is also formed when any substance containing hydrogen is burned. The hydrogen combines chemically with the oxygen in the air to form water molecules—chemical symbol, H_2O (2 atoms of hydrogen, 1 atom of oxygen). Any kind of COMBUSTION—wood, fire, gas flame, burning candle—results in the formation of water vapor. Every gallon (3.8 liters) of gas burned in a car engine produces 7 pints (3.3 liters) of water—which can be seen streaming from the exhaust on a cool day.   H.W.M.

SEE ALSO: ATMOSPHERE, EVAPORATION, WATER CYCLE, WEATHER

Water vascular system The water vascular system is found in the body of the STARFISH and other similar animals (the *echinoderms*). It is used to move the animal from place to place. The system is made of canals, valves, and tube feet. It works by means of water pressure.

On the upper surface of a starfish, a sieve-like *madreporite* takes in sea water. This

Buchsbaum

The tube feet of a starfish are part of the water vascular system

opening is connected by a stone canal to a circular canal around the mouth. From the circular canal, radial canals enter the arms. Lateral canals run from the radial canals to tube feet. Tube feet are cylinders of tissue with longitudinal muscles in their walls. On their inner ends are sacs (*ampullae*) with circular muscles, while on the outer ends are suckers.

Water enters ampullae through the madreporite and canal system. When ampullae contract, the water in them is prevented from returning to the radial canals by valves. It is forced under pressure into the tube feet. The feet attach themselves to sea-bottom surfaces with their suckers. In order to release the suckers, the longitudinal muscles contract and force the water back into the ampullae. By the joint action of the starfish's many tube feet, the animal moves forward.   J. C. K.

SEE ALSO: ECHINODERMATA

Waterfall Waterfalls occur where water drops suddenly from a high point of ground to a lower point. Waterfalls are enjoyed for their beauty and interesting effects. There are many different conditions which may lead to the formation of a waterfall.

One of these conditions is present when a stream passes over a more resistant rock to one less resistant. EROSION is more rapid in the less resistant formation, so a cliff or steep slope develops. The Great Falls of the Yellowstone River in Wyoming were created in this way.

In some cases, undermining causes unsupported rocks to break away to develop steep

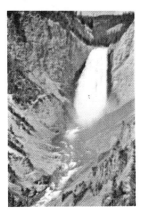

The great power behind a waterfall can be "harnessed" for hydroelectricity
Courtesy Society For Visual Education, Inc.

slopes or cliffs. Niagara Falls is an example of this phenomenon. There are also some cases where certain tributary streams join their main stream by plunging over steep cliffs.

Where there is an uplifting of fault blocks, waterfalls are common. They are also formed in regions that were once covered with glaciers. Due to glacial action, the main valleys have been dug deeper than their tributaries. Then when the ice disappears, the water flows down the steep slopes that mark the boundaries between tributary valley and main valleys.   V. V. N.
SEE ALSO: DAM, HYDROELECTRIC POWER

Watermelon see Melon

Watershed A watershed is the land on which rain falls and then drains or runs into a RIVER. On a roof, the incline of the roof indicates which way the water will run off. Mountains and land elevations also direct the course of running water. This is called a *watershed*.
SEE ALSO: CONTINENTAL DIVIDE

Waterspout A waterspout occurs at sea. It has a tornado-like appearance, except that it seems to descend from a cloud. At one time the waterspout was thought to be a great column of water and extremely dangerous. Now it is known that the waterspout is primarily cloud-like. It seldom lasts for over 30 minutes, and is not very dangerous.

A waterspout is caused when the surface of the water is heated to a high temperature. Intense air currents begin to move in opposite directions about each other in a whirlpool fashion. The swirling winds form a spiraling cloud which has a low pressure center. Water vapor is sucked into the center, creating the spout-like appearance.

Though waterspouts are usually only a few hundred feet or meters high and 20 to 30 feet (6 to 9 meters) in diameter, they disrupt the sea so that great quantities of spray are thrown up to the tip of the spout. Because of the earth's rotation, they travel across the seas counterclockwise in the Northern Hemisphere and clockwise (the opposite direction) in the Southern Hemisphere.   D.J.I.
SEE ALSO: AIR MASSES, ATMOSPHERE, EARTH, WIND

Watson, James D. (1928-   ) Watson is a U.S. biochemist who shared in the 1962 NOBEL PRIZE in physiology and medicine with Francis Crick and Maurice Wilkins. Their combined research led to the discovery of the molecular structure of DNA. DNA carries genetic information from generation to generation.

Based on the X-ray diffraction data of Wilkins and the known stereochemical configurations possible for such a molecule, Watson and Crick were able to construct a molecular model of DNA (deoxyribonucleic acid). It shows DNA to be a double helix with the bases forming the core, the sugar, and phosphate groups are on the outside of the molecule. DNA carries all the data needed to determine the total appearance and function of an organism.   P.P.S.
SEE ALSO: DNA

Watt A watt is a unit of power — usually electrical power. This unit was named for James Watt, the inventor of the steam engine. Although the watt is the standard unit of power in the metric system of MEASUREMENT, the kilowatt (1000 watts) is more generally used.

A watt is that amount of power used when a force of one newton acts through a distance of one meter in one second of time. In electrical terms the watt is equal to the power developed when one AMPERE flows under a pressure of one VOLT.   M.S.
SEE ALSO: ELECTRICITY, ENERGY, KILOWATT HOUR, POWER, WATT-HOUR METER

Watt, James (1736-1819) James Watt was a Scottish engineer who invented the modern condensing steam ENGINE. In reality, there had been a number of steam engines invented before Watt's time, but they used such quantities of steam that they were impractical. James Watt invented a condenser that reduced the amount of steam needed. The *watt,* a measure of power, was named for him.

Watt was born in Greenock, Scotland, January 19, 1736. At the age of thirteen he showed exceptional ability in mathematics and became known as an outstanding student of the subject. In 1756 he went to the University of Glasgow to serve as mathematical instrument maker for its mathematics and science departments, and there Watt became interested in steam engines.

After he had been at the university for almost eight years, Watt was asked to repair a model of the Newcomen steam engine. The tremendous amount of steam used by the model aroused him, and he resolved to invent a more efficient machine. He reasoned that if a cylinder and vacuum were connected, steam would rush into the vacuum and there it could be condensed without cooling the cylinder.

In 1774 Watt and Matthew Boulton formed a business partnership and organized a company to manufacture engines. The business was an immediate success. Thereafter, James Watt was financially able to carry out scientific research and to work on the invention of many machines and parts of machines. He proved that water is not an element, but a compound substance. D. H. J.

Watt-hour meter A watt-hour meter is a device which measures and registers electric power usage during a period of time. This meter should not be confused with a *wattmeter,* an instrument that measures the amount of electric power at any instant.

The most common watt-hour meter is the familiar glass-enclosed device attached to most houses. This meter, called an *induction-type* watt-hour meter, has the same basic parts as other specialized watt-hour meters;

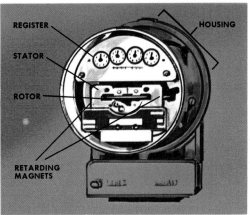

The watt-hour meter commonly found in homes has four dials that work on a ratio of 10 to 1. The first moves around ten times while the second moves once.

the difference is the method of applying electricity through the meter circuit. The parts are: *stator, rotor, retarding magnets, register,* and *meter housing.*

Induction-type meters measure alternating current electricity. Incoming electricity, passed through the stator, causes the rotor to revolve, as in the operation of an electric motor. Windings (wire) in the stator relate the particular combination of voltage and current to the speed of rotation. The retarding magnets control the rotor speed to keep it proportional to the power. The more watts consumed, the faster the rotor turns.

Through a gear train the rotor turns four dials in the register. The dials indicate how many kilowatt hours (1000 watt-hours) have been consumed. By reading the meter, and subtracting from that reading the previous measurement, the electric company can determine how much electricity has been used.   E. I. D.

SEE ALSO: KILOWATT HOUR

Wave A wave may be described as the traveling process of ENERGY through a body of matter without that matter being carried along with it. A wave is a periodic process, that is, one in which the same operations are repeated over and over again. Sound, heat, and light, as well as electromagnetic and other radiation impulses, travel in waves.

There are three kinds of waves. *Mechanical waves* occur when energy is carried by stresses in a liquid or solid body. Water waves and the waves along the strings of a musical instrument are mechanical waves. *Sound waves* occur when energy is carried through

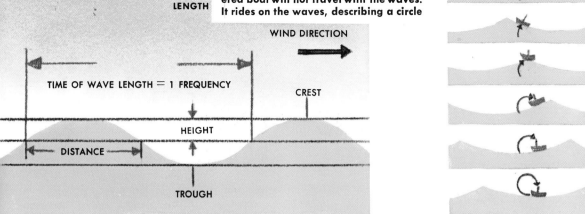

SPEED OF WAVES = FREQUENCY × WAVE LENGTH

Right: Like water particles, a non-powered boat will not travel with the waves. It rides on the waves, describing a circle

WIND DIRECTION

TIME OF WAVE LENGTH = 1 FREQUENCY

CREST

HEIGHT

DISTANCE

TROUGH

a gas, generally air, by layers of low and high pressure moving along alternately. *Electromagnetic waves* consist of *electric* and *magnetic fields* which exchange energy as they move through an electrically insulated material or through empty space. X rays, light, and radio waves are examples of electromagnetic waves.

The essence of a wave process would seem to be the periodic interchange of energy from the *potential* into the *kinetic* form and back again, continually. The number of times per second that such an interchange of energy occurs is called the *frequency* of the wave. The speed with which energy is carried through the system by the wave is called the VELOCITY of the wave. The distance through which the energy moves during the time of one interchange (from kinetic to potential) is called the *wavelength*. The *intensity* of a wave may be measured in terms of the amount of energy or power carried through one square unit of area perpendicular to the direction of wave motion. These may be considered to be general properties of *all* wave systems.

Ocean waves are caused by earthquakes, tides, and winds. Wind-driven waves are the most familiar. When the wind blows across the water surface, it pushes the water up into "rows" followed by depressions. The peaks of the wave are called the *crests,* and the depressions are *troughs.* Half the distance between crest and trough is the height.

Waves can rise to a height of only ⅐ of their length before spilling over into whitecaps. It is clear, therefore, that the highest waves result from the longest fetches. (The fetch means the unobstructed distance over which the wind blows.) Waves in the Atlantic rarely reach more than 40 feet (12 meters); in the Pacific, seldom more than 50 feet (15 meters).

Although waves appear to carry water with them, actually only 1 percent of the water is transported during heavy seas. Water particles only appear to travel.

Much has been learned about waves, but much research remains to be done before they are fully understood.   R. N. J.

SEE ALSO: CURRENTS, OCEAN; LIGHT; RADIATION; RADIO; SHORT WAVE; QUANTUM THEORY; STANDING WAVE; TIDE

Wax Wax, originally called *beeswax,* is any of various semi-solid, large molecule, HYDROCARBON substances produced by plants, bees or other animals, or by chemical means.

Waxwing, cedar The cedar waxwing is a beautiful, crested bird about 7¼ inches (18.4 centimeters) long. Its cinnamon-brown plumage shades to gray or chestnut and is marked by black, white, and yellow. Red, waxlike drops on its wing feathers distinguish it from almost all birds. It has a black, wedge-shaped patch from the beak to back of the eye.

The cedar waxwing cannot sing, but makes a few high-pitched hissing notes. It feeds on small fruits and insects caught on the wing. Its bulky nest is usually built in orchards. The female lays from three to five bluish-gray eggs marked with brown or purple spots. Cedar waxwings are generally found in temperate North America, and may migrate to the West Indies.   D. C. H.

Cedar waxwing

Weapons Weapons are devices used in offensive or defensive fighting to destroy, defeat, or injure an enemy. Offensive types of weapons are also used for hunting game to provide food for man.

Defensive weapons, such as a shield, a bullet-proof vest, or a bomb shelter, are used for protection. This article, as most discussions of weapons, deals only with offensive weapons—those which reach out and strike the enemy, such as a spear, a gun, or a bomb.

The first weapon was probably the stone thrown by hand. Primitive man must have discovered early that by placing the stone in a sling, more distance and greater impact were attainable. Later, he shaped stones and used them as spearheads. Sometimes he imbedded stones in the trunks of young trees. When the trees had grown firmly around the stones, he cut the tree above and below the stones to produce sturdy stone axes. Eventually man was to develop the bow, using stones for arrowheads.

About 5,000 B.C., copper, which was one of the first metals known to man, was first mined in the uncombined state. After this discovery until about 1000 B.C., spearheads, arrowheads, knives, and swords were made of copper or its alloy, bronze. Iron, which was discovered about the same time that bronze was first made, was soon used to replace bronze in weapons.

The composite bow, a powerful variation of the bow, was developed in Asia. This bow was made of three different materials bonded together to provide a strong spring action. Bows of this type usually had a reflex action—when the bow was strung, it bent in the direction opposite to that when unstrung.

From 200 B.C. to 400 A.D., the Romans made a great contribution to the development of war engines. They invented the battering ram, catapults (giant slingshots), and fighting towers.

During the medieval centuries, refinements of older weapons continued. The long bow (5 to 6 feet or 1.5 to 1.8 meters long) became popular because of its greater penetration and accuracy. The more powerful crossbow was also developed.

GUNPOWDER was first used to fire cannons in early 1300 A.D. The early cannons were made of wood and fired large spears. Gradually, metal cannons came into use. The earlier models fired stones; the later ones fired lead balls. Smaller versions of the cannon were held in the hands. Burning ropes and hot iron rods were used to set off the gunpowder in these devices. Hand guns were improved during the 16th century with the invention of the *matchlock,* a device which automatically ignited the powder each time the trigger was pressed. Variations of igniters included both stone and metal spark makers.

As cannons were perfected, they became more useful on board ships. In early 1500, special short-barreled cannons, called *mortars,* were designed to fire at a steep angle and drop their charges on the target. From 1500 to 1700, mobile artillery pieces were developed. By use of protractors and levels, cannons were aimed for effective firing. Bombs also came into use during this period. Instead of a solid metal ball, a hollow sphere filled with explosive material was fired from the cannon.

In the early 1600's, the Germans invented the basic rifle as it is known today. Instead of having a smooth bore like other hand guns, a spiral, or rifled, groove was cut into the barrel. When a slightly oversized ball was forced out of the barrel, it threaded its way along the spiral and continued to spin after it left the muzzle. The spin maintained an accurate line of fire, whereas a PROJECTILE without spin wobbled and followed an unpredictable trajectory. The Kentucky rifle, developed from the German design, was of smaller bore diameter and lighter in weight. It had a flintlock (flint striking steel) firing mechanism and a leather-covered bullet that was easier to insert into the rifled bore. It was accurate up to 100 yards (91.4 meters).

About 1800, a major change in loading rifles occurred. Until this time, charges were rammed down the barrel from the muzzle end of the gun. The *breechloading* rifle, loading from the firing-chamber end of the barrel, was invented. Also the percussion principle of firing gunpowder was developed. By striking a sharp blow to a mild but sensitive explosive, the gunpowder could be

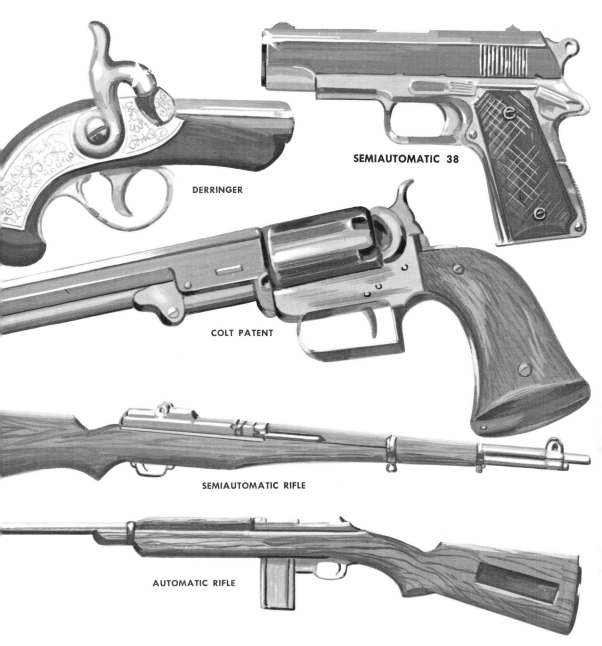

DERRINGER

SEMIAUTOMATIC 38

COLT PATENT

SEMIAUTOMATIC RIFLE

AUTOMATIC RIFLE

ignited. The matchlock was thus no longer needed.

The French Minie balls replaced the round lead balls because of their improved performance. Although called a ball, it was the first streamlined bullet that proved practical.

Small handguns or pistols found a good market in the 19th century. One of the most famous was the Derringer. Colt's Patent Revolver, invented in 1836, was one of the first successful, repeating action guns. It is the forerunner of present-day hand guns. In the latter half of the 1800's, bullets with self-contained primers were invented. The expanding gases of the explosion forced the wall of the shell tightly against the chamber to prevent the loss of its pressure. The hol-

low base of the bullet also expanded and followed the spiral riflings down the barrel. This cartridge principle is now used on all guns except for large cannons.

Small arms—.60 caliber (diameter of projectile in inches) and under—have developed rapidly during the past 100 years. Automatic pistols became popular after 1900 when revolvers remained relatively unchanged. Rifles progressed from single shot to repeaters. The armed forces now use semi-automatic and fully automatic rifles. A semi-automatic rifle fires each time the trigger is pulled. The explosive gas pressure is utilized to load the next cartridge. An automatic rifle continues to fire as long as the trigger is pressed and the supply of bullets holds out.

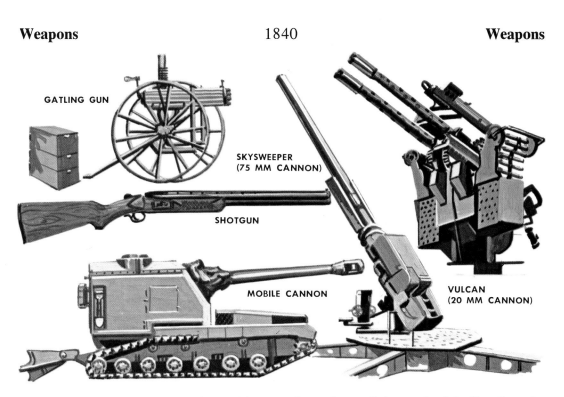

GATLING GUN

SKYSWEEPER
(75 MM CANNON)

SHOTGUN

MOBILE CANNON

VULCAN
(20 MM CANNON)

Shotguns use paper-covered cartridges that contain many small balls, or "shot." The shot spreads out over a relatively large area, and is often used for hunting small game.

Another type of small arms developed within the century is the machine gun. This gun fires great quantities of ammunition in a short time. The Gatling gun, developed during the Civil War and used in the Spanish War, was operated by a hand crank. The crank rotated ten barrels past one firing point so that a firing rate of 800 shots per minute could be attained. This principle is used today on jet fighter aircraft—the Vulcan cannon can fire 6000 rounds of 20 mm. ammunition per minute. Some machine guns are light enough to be carried by one man; however, two-man teams are not uncommon for moving these weapons. Most common machine guns have a single barrel, and work the same as the automatic rifle in principle; however, they use more ammunition and can fire for longer periods. Through World War II and the Korean War, machine guns were the main protective armament of all aircraft. Rockets and guided missiles have become standard armament in place of machine guns.

Cannons, defined as guns over .60 caliber, have similarly improved in operating efficiency during the past century. Rifling and copper-banded shells have made muzzle load-ing and smooth bores obsolete. Recoil mechanisms for absorbing the shock when firing weapons were one of the more desirable improvements. The early coastal defense guns were counterweighted so they could be raised into firing position. When they were fired, the tremendous recoil was damped by large piston-type shock absorbers. Various combinations of springs, hydraulic pistons, and compressed gases are now used to absorb recoil and return the gun barrel to firing position.

The armored machine gun destroyer, better known as a *tank*, became prominent during World War I. Armed with machine guns and protecting its crew with heavy armor plate, a tank could penetrate almost any enemy line at the time. Modern tanks carry cannons as well as machine guns. Anti-tank weapons include the hand grenade and portable rocket launchers.

Guided missiles have replaced cannons on most aircraft, gunboats, and in the field. Most guided missiles are powered by a rocket engine and guided to their targets using computers and other guidance systems. Ballistic missiles, such as an *intercontinental ballistic missile* (ICBM) can strike a target from about 3,400 to 8,000 miles (5,500 to 13,000 km) away. Many ICBMs were built by the U.S. and the Soviet Union during the Cold War, which ended in the early 1990s. The United States Army's Pershing missiles, medium-range ballistic missiles, can generally fly from 100 to

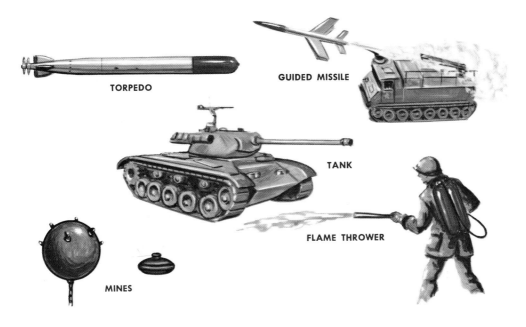

TORPEDO

GUIDED MISSILE

TANK

FLAME THROWER

MINES

400 miles (160 to 640 km).

Most guided missiles are nonballistic missiles. Cruise missiles are one example. These jet-powered missiles are launched from the ground, from large aircraft, and from submarines. They can fly at extremely low altitude to avoid radar detection. Other missile types include surface-to-surface missiles (SSMs), surface-to-air missiles (SAMs) and air-to-air missiles.

Missiles designed to be used against approaching enemy missiles are called *anti-missile missiles*. One type, known as *antiballistic missiles* (ABMs) is used against enemy ballistic missiles. The U.S. Army's *Patriot* missile is an example of an ABM.

Some missiles carry nuclear bombs. Aerial bombs were first used in World War I, when light-weight explosives were dropped by hand from aircraft. Another type of bomb, the torpedo, was designed for underwater demolition of ships.

Other weapons include mines, flame-throwers, and grenades. Mines are a form of explosive floated on water or hidden on land. They explode when approached or touched. Flamethrowers, both portable and tank-mounted, shoot streams of burning gasoline and oil into places where ordinary firearms cannot penetrate. Grenades are small missiles that contain explosives or chemicals.

E.I.D./M.K.H.

SEE ALSO: BOMBS, EXPLOSIVES, MISSILE, NUCLEAR ENERGY, ROCKET

Weasel The weasel is a slender, furry animal that eats mice, rats, moles, and insects. It is related to the wolverine, skunk, badger and otter.

Weasels are swift, brave animals. They are good hunters with abounding energy and a sharp sense of sight and smell. They can chase their prey up trees, through holes in the ground, and into the water because they are excellent swimmers.

For its young the weasel makes nests of twigs and leaves in hollow trees or in holes in the ground. The mother will fight fiercely and courageously to protect the young.

There are many varieties of the weasel family, called Mustelidae. They range in length from 10 to 36 inches (25.4 to 91.4 centimeters), and inhabit North America and northern Europe and Asia. All of the species have a long slender body, short legs, a small head, and sharp nose. The teeth are sharp. They can climb, swim, and move with tremendous speed.

Only the typical weasels, which include the common *American weasel* and the *European ermine,* change color of fur through the seasons for camouflage. The summer *pelage*

All photos J. W. Thompson

The summer coat of the American weasel is called *stoat*

During the winter the coat turns white but keeps the black tail, and the animal is known by its familiar name, the *ermine*

Some mink fur takes on a special tint of brown and is called the platinum mink

The rare Fisher weasel is very similar to the martens

or coat, is dark brown or tawny, shaded to black, with black tail tip and yellowish white undersides. At this time the animal is called a *stoat*. In its white winter coat it is called an *ermine*. The winter coat is the traditional lining and decoration of royal ceremonial robes. The European ermine's fur is superior to that of the North American weasel. The color change does not occur in warmer climates; weasels living south of a constant snow cover will remain brown throughout the winter. The black tip of the tail never changes color. The typical weasel grows to a length of 10 inches (25.4 centimeters) for the European ermine and 24 inches (61 centimeters) for the American weasel.

A close relative of the weasel and approximately of the same size is the *ferret*. Its coat is yellowish brown with black feet. This species is common in the western United States. A type of albino ferret has been domesticated in Europe and used in hunting. Closely related to the ferret is the *polecat*. This European weasel is about 24 inches (61 centimeters) long, with dark brownish fur on the back, black fur underneath and white markings on the head. The name is derived from *poultry cat*, as it preys on poultry.

The aristocrat of the fur-bearing weasel is the *sable*, particularly the Russian sable. This animal grows to 28 inches (71.1 centimeters) long. The soft, heavy coat is brown the year around, and is much in demand for fine furs. The smaller *red sable* of Siberia has buff and tawny fur.

The *mink*, also of the weasel family, is best known in the United States and Canada. It has been domesticated and is raised successfully on fur farms. Selective breeding has developed many beautiful shadings in the color of the coat. The American mink and the *kolinsky*, an Asiatic mink, grow to a length of 18 to 24 inches (45.7 to 61 centimeters).

The *Pacific marten* and the *pine marten* are larger members of the Mustelidae family. Their habitat is the Pacific northwest, and because of indiscriminate trapping they are fast becoming extinct. The European variety is called the *stone marten*.

One of the largest of the weasels, and by far the most intelligent, is the *fisher*. At one time these animals abounded in New England and New York State but they, too, are fast disappearing.   J.M.C.

SEE ALSO: BADGER, OTTER, SKUNK

Lightning is one of the most spectacular weather phenomena. It is caused by the attraction between negative and positive charges in the clouds

Courtesy Society For Visual Education, Inc.

Weather Weather is the physical condition of our environment. Weather includes the temperature, humidity, wind, and air pressure. Weather can help us or hurt us. Floods and hurricanes cause millions of dollars of damage each year. There is an average of 593 tornadoes, and 6,000 hail, lightning, wind, and thunderstorms each year. No wonder that everyone talks about the weather!

There are different weather conditions each day. These are the temperature of the air, the humidity, the direction and speed of the wind, the amount of clouds, and any rain or snow. The one element of weather hardly noticeable is the air pressure. But this is one of the most important, since daily changes in all the other elements depend on pressure changes. All these elements must be considered together to give the current conditions of the atmosphere which is called weather.

The layer of air around the earth is the *atmosphere* and is both compressible and invisible. The atmosphere is a mixture of about 78% nitrogen, 21% oxygen, and 1% other minor gases. Water, which is called WATER VAPOR in the gaseous state, is always present in variable amounts.

The atmosphere is held to the earth by the force of gravity and, therefore, has weight. The barometer is used to measure the weight of air in units of pressure called *millibars*.

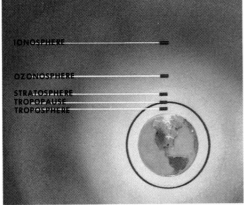

The average sea level pressure is 1013.2 millibars. Pressure readings are taken at many places, since the daily weather patterns are caused by the general easterly movement of high and low pressure air masses.

There is no definite upper limit of the atmosphere, and small amounts of air are found several hundred miles above the earth. Most of the air, however, is compressed to within about 50 miles (80.5 kilometers) of the earth's surface. The layer of air nearest the ground is called the *troposphere* and extends to a height of about 5 miles (8 kilometers) above the North and South poles and to 11 miles (17.7 kilometers) above the equator. In this layer the temperature decreases at the average rate of 1° F. for each 300 feet of altitude (or about .4° C. for each 100 meters). Almost all the weather affecting the earth develops in this layer of air.

Above the troposphere is the *stratosphere* in which there is very little moisture, and the temperature is nearly constant. The stratosphere extends to about 50 miles (80.5 kilometers) above the earth. Temperatures in this layer average about -70° F. (-56° C.).

Near the ground, the temperature of the air is measured by thermometers placed in small shelters about 4 feet (1.2 meters) above sod. The shelter has *louvered* sides to allow air to circulate past the thermometers but prevents the temperature from being affected by the sun's rays, and rain or snow. In the United States, surface temperatures have ranged from an extreme maximum of 134° F. (56.7° C.) to a minimum of -66° F. (-23° C.).

Wind is the motion of air over the earth's surface and results from variations in air pressure. Winds tend to blow from areas of high pressure to areas of low pressure. The greater the difference in pressure between two areas, the greater the force of the wind. One would expect the wind to blow directly from high pressure to low pressure in the same manner as water flows down a hill. But because of the rotation of the earth, the general rotation of winds is clockwise in the Northern Hemisphere and counterclockwise in the Southern Hemisphere. This effect is expressed in the famous *Buys Ballot's Law of Winds,* which states that an observer facing the wind in the Northern Hemisphere has lower pressure on the right (the low is reversed in the Southern Hemisphere).

Courtesy Society For Visual Education, Inc.

If the earth did not revolve on its axis, all winds would run north and south

On a hot summer day one often hears the expression, "It's not the heat; it's the humidity." HUMIDITY refers to the invisible water vapor that is always present in the atmosphere. Water vapor gets into the air by evaporation from the water in rivers, lakes, oceans, and other sources such as plants and animals. As the temperature of the air rises, the amount of water vapor it can hold increases. However, there is a maximum amount the air can hold for any given temperature. When this maximum point is reached, the air is said to be *saturated*. The temperature at which the air reaches saturation is called the *dew point*.

At the saturation point, some of the invisible water vapor begins to condense into liquid water. This process of condensation in the atmosphere is not fully understood but

Water vapor condenses on a dust particle

Courtesy Society For Visual Education, Inc.

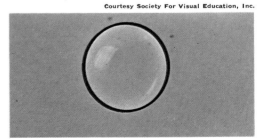

Cirrus clouds (top) may form at high altitudes when the dew point is below freezing

Cumulus clouds form by rising air currents and tend to produce storms

N

W

Stratus clouds form in moist air near the ground below a temperature inversion

E

A tornado is a whirling wind with a funnel-shaped cloud. It moves in a narrow path

S

"The air moves like a river and carries the clouds with it"
—Leonardo da Vinci

seems to depend on the presence of small particles of dust, salt, smoke, and other solid materials. These tiny particles are called *condensation nuclei,* and their size varies from $\frac{1}{1000}$ to $1/10$ of a millimeter. The water vapor in the air condenses on these small particles to form small cloud droplets.

Another interesting property of water is its ability to remain in a liquid state at temperatures well below the freezing point. In this state the water is said to be *supercooled.* Liquid water has been found in clouds with temperatures as low as -40° F. (-40° C.). This means that in the higher levels of clouds, where the temperature is below freezing, there are likely to be large amounts of supercooled water in addition to some ice crystals.

The clouds formed by the condensation process are of three basic types: the high streak clouds called *cirrus;* the clouds in layers called *stratus;* and the tower, or pile, clouds called *cumulus.*

The cirrus clouds are found in the high levels of the troposphere and are composed of ice crystals. They appear, many times, as long streaks across the blue sky and cause the halos around the sun and moon.

Stratus clouds are developed by cooling of a layer of air to below the dew point temperature. If the cooling occurs close to ground, the cloud is in the form of fog. Stratus clouds are formed along sea coasts and lake shores when the air is cooled by moving over the colder water surface. This type of cloud is also formed when rain is falling through a layer of unsaturated air. The evaporation of some of the raindrops into water vapor cools this layer below the dew point, and a stratus cloud develops.

Cumulus clouds develop from the cooling of rising air currents by mixing with the colder air at high levels and by expansion of the air at lower pressure. Cumulus clouds tend to grow upward, and many tower to heights of 6 miles (9.7 kilometers) or higher. From such towering clouds, showers will fall; and thunderstorms, hail, and even tornadoes develop.

A large cumulus cloud may contain an amount of cloud droplets and ice crystals weighing as much as 100,000 tons (91,000 metric tons). The droplets and ice crystals are so small, however, that the motion of the air holds the particles in suspension.

Courtesy Society For Visual Education, Inc.

Topographical conditions can affect the weather.

Not until the cloud drops grow to a size of 1/10 to 1 millimeter in diameter will they be able to fall to the ground. It has been estimated that it takes a million cloud drops to equal one raindrop.

The growth from the small cloud drop to a raindrop seems to depend on having a large amount of supercooled water and some ice crystals in clouds with temperatures well below the freezing point. The supercooled water tends to join the ice crystals and grow into a snowflake. The falling snowflake, in reaching a layer of air with temperature above freezing, will melt and fall to the ground as a raindrop. During cold winter weather, the snowflakes will fall to the ground without melting, while in spring it is not uncommon to have a mixture of rain and snow at the same time.

This process of rain formation is usually found in the temperate zone, but heavy showers develop in the tropics from clouds that have temperatures above the freezing point. In such cases, it is believed that the raindrops form because of collision of the cloud drops in violent, vertical currents.

Man's knowledge of all the elements of weather and the motion of the atmosphere is still incomplete. Meteorology, the science of weather, is making rapid progress in various research fields in order that man may arrive at a better understanding of the weather—the changes in temperature, wind, pressure, and moisture.   C. B. J.

SEE ALSO: ATMOSPHERE, PRECIPITATION (WEATHER), SEASONS, WEATHER MAP

Weather Service, National Nearly everyone listens to the weather forecasts on radio and television, or reads the forecasts in daily newspapers. In the U.S., the National Weather Service provides many of these forecasts, as well as observations and records of the weather in the U.S. and its territories. It also sends out warnings of hurricanes, tornadoes, and severe storms, and issues special weather information for farmers and pilots.

The United States weather service was first organized by Congress on February 9, 1870. At that time, it was known as the United States Weather Bureau. In 1891, the Weather Bureau became a unit of the Department of Agriculture. In 1965, Congress made the Weather Bureau part of the Environmental Science Service Administration, a branch of the Department of Commerce. The bureau was renamed the National Weather Service in 1970, when it became part of the National Oceanic and Atmospheric Administration.

The Weather Service has its central office in Washington, D.C., and regional offices around the U.S. Observation stations, radar, satellites, and computers keep a 24-hour watch on the environment. Data from these systems is collected by local weather stations, which send them to the Weather Service's National Meteorological Center near Washington, D.C. The center's staff analyzes the reports and uses high-speed computers to make forecasts, which are then sent to local offices.

Special forecast centers, such as the Severe Local Storm Center in Kansas City, Missouri, watch for and issue warnings about storms, hurricanes, and floods that may endanger life and property. Weather advice, warnings, and general forecasts are given to the public by means of newspapers, radio, television, tele-

© Tom Dietrich

A meteorologist at work

phone, and computer networks. The National Weather Service also collects and distributes weather data on climate and water conditions for navigation, aviation, shipping, and the military.

In the early 1990s, the National Weather Service began implementing a $4.5 billion modernization plan. Part of the plan called for the installation of more than a hundred Doppler radars (see WEATHER STATION, RADAR) around the U.S. by 1996. The first three systems were in operation in 1993. Also in varying degrees of completion in 1993 were hundreds of automated weather stations capable of measuring many weather elements without the presence of human workers. The first in a new generation of weather satellites was scheduled to be sent into orbit in 1994. New and more powerful supercomputers, software, and communication procedures will be used to process an increasing flow of data.

M.K.H.

SEE ALSO: INTERNATIONAL GEOPHYSICAL YEAR, WEATHER, WEATHER FORECASTING

Weather forecasting The rotation of the earth and heat from the sun cause motion in the ATMOSPHERE and changes in weather. Describing these changes, and predicting new changes is called weather forecasting. Scientists who forecast the weather are called *meteorologists.*

Forecasting the weather is a sophisticated and complex process, but it is an important one. Farmers need to know about rainfall and temperature so they can plan their crops. Pilots need to know about wind speed and direction to determine how much fuel they will need in a flight. People in towns and cities need to know about hurricanes, tornadoes, and floods so they can protect their property and their lives.

Many weather forecasts in the United States are prepared by the National Weather Service. Meteorologists collect data on weather conditions throughout the world. They use this information to draw WEATHER MAPS that show the AIR PRESSURE, wind, temperature, cloud

Weather forecasts warn people of tornadoes and other weather threats.

© Harold N. Lambert/SuperStock Intl.

Automated weather stations collect data that is used to monitor and predict weather. Above, a technician adjusts a rain gauge that is fenced in to protect it from wind currents.

© Tom Dietrich

cover, and moisture in various areas. The maps are analyzed and used to prepare the actual forecast. Some forecasts are good for a 24-hour period, while others are accurate for up to a week.

In general, the three steps needed to prepare a forecast are: (1) data collection, (2) data analysis, and (3) forecasting.

DATA COLLECTION

Modern weather forecasting depends on continuous observations and accurate measurements of weather conditions. Many of these observations are made at weather stations. Weather stations are located all over the world in cities, at airports, on ships, and in isolated locations such as remote islands and the North and South Poles.

Each weather observation consists of measuring a variety of weather elements, such as air pressure, pressure changes in the past three hours, temperature, air moisture (humidity), wind direction, and wind speed. Notes are also made about the amount and type of precipitation, the degree of visibility,

and cloud cover.

Observations of the upper air are made every day using *weather balloons*. These balloons carry instruments called *radiosondes* that record and transmit data about the temperature, moisture, and winds of the atmosphere. The data is sent back to the weather station by radio transmission.

Many stations use RADAR to receive signals reflecting from rain, snow, and hail. A *radarscope* shows where the precipitation is falling and the location and velocity of storms. In addition, stations gather data from *weather satellites*, which orbit earth. These satellites carry television cameras that take pictures of clouds above the earth. The pictures are used by the National Weather Service to aid in predicting when and where storms will occur.

An agency of the United Nations, called the World Meteorological Organization (WMO), helps coordinate the efforts of the independent stations by collecting and distributing information by means of a worldwide communications network. The data is fed into powerful supercomputers, which can perform millions of calculations per second.

ESA/Eumetsat

In the last half of the twentieth century, satellites have kept a close watch on the planet. The new GOES-I weather satellite (left) is scheduled to be launched in 1994.

AA/NWS

ANALYSIS

The information collected by weather stations, weather balloons, and satellites is used to make weather maps. In the United States, these maps are prepared by computers at the National Weather Service offices. The computers create the maps by solving complex mathematical formulas that use the observations as a starting point.

Several different types of maps and charts are produced from the weather observations. *Temperature charts* indicate the highest and lowest surface temperatures in various places over a 24-hour period. *Precipitation charts* show where precipitation occurred during a 24-hour period.

Some maps show atmospheric conditions, such as high-level winds, temperatures, and air moisture. The *500-millibar chart* is the most commonly used version of this type of map. It shows the temperature, wind direction and speed, and humidity that were measured at an altitude of 18,400 feet (5,608 meters). At this altitude, the air pressure equals half the average air pressure at sea level.

Surface weather maps show the weather conditions that were measured at the earth's surface at a certain time of the day. These maps are also called *synoptic charts* (synoptic means "seen together").

Surface weather maps contain a number of long, curving lines, called *contour lines.* There are usually two different types of contour lines on a surface map: *isotherms* and *isobars.* Isotherms connect points that have the same temperature. Isobars connect points that have the same air pressure. The areas linked by low-pressure isobars show places where the air pressure is low. These areas are called *depressions.* Low air pressure tends to bring wind, clouds, and rain. The areas linked by high-pressure isobars show places where the air pressure is high. Areas of high pressure usually indicate dry, settled weather. Surface maps also show precipitation as shaded areas.

FORECASTING

Meteorologists analyze the various weather maps and charts to prepare their forecasts. *A forecast map* is created that shows all the

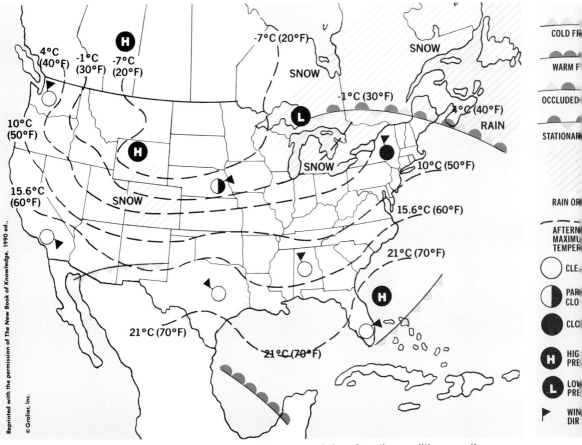

This simplified form of a synoptic map gives a general view of weather conditions over the United States on a particular day. Almost at a glance, you can see how temperatures varied from one part of the country to another and what areas had snow or rain.

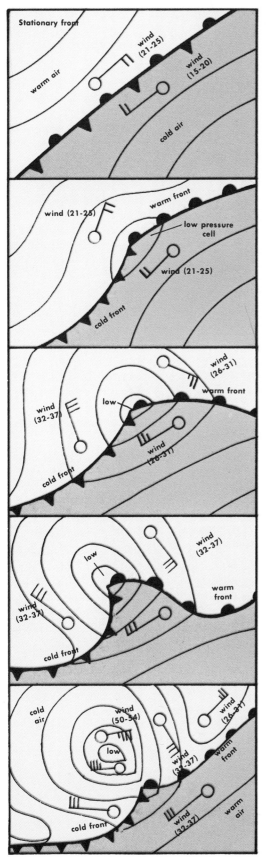

Series of weather maps showing how warm and cold fronts influence weather. The last map shows how the fully developed low causes high winds and stormy conditions as the fronts pass through.

Weather forecasting

important weather conditions—high and low pressure centers, fronts, air masses, and precipitation areas—as they are expected to appear in 24 or 36 hours. The forecast maps help show a picture of what future weather conditions will be like based on the current surface weather reports, wind circulation patterns, and the movement of storm fronts.

These maps are updated several times a day as new weather data is received. The reason for this is that no two forecast maps are identical: In one case, a frontal zone may produce heavy showers, in another, only brief cloudiness. The temperatures of air masses constantly change, and the intensity of a storm center can change quite rapidly.

Meteorologists use the forecast map to create written and verbal predictions of what the weather will be like during the forecast period. These predictions are not always accurate. Some inaccuracies are due to lack of data. Others are due to the fact that much is still unknown about the atmosphere and how weather develops. The mathematical equations that are used to describe the atmospheric motions are very complex, and only approximate solutions can be used. The final forecast depends a great deal on the experience and knowledge of the forecaster.

Thousands of meteorologists and other scientists are involved in forecasting the weather in the U.S. alone. In the early 1990s, the U.S. Weather Service began building automated stations that could measure and transmit many weather conditions without onsite human observers. The action prompted a 1992 lawsuit by unionized meteorologists. In some cases, the automated stations work well. But errors can occur. A U.S. Government Accounting Office report indicated that "the precipitation identification sensor currently mistakes insects and spider webs for precipitation."

The economic value of knowing future weather conditions is very important to agriculture, commerce, and industry. Large cities must ready snow-removal equipment before snow begins to fall so that highways can be kept open and safe for travel. Severe storm warnings help prevent loss of life and reduce property loss. Military operations require knowledge of present and future weather conditions. These demands have led to a wide variety of forecasts.

Public forecasts are issued every six hours to inform the public of weather conditions expected during the next two days. These forecasts include temperature, degree of cloud-iness, precipitation, and wind conditions. The chance of rain or snow is also given in these forecasts by use of probability figures. A probability of 70 percent means that most places will have some precipitation. On the other hand, probability of less than 20 percent indicates that rain or snow is unlikely. Forecasts for five-day periods are prepared three times a week to indicate general changes in temperature and precipitation. A nation-wide forecast for a month is prepared by the National Weather Service in Washington.

Aviation forecasts are available through-out the country and for overseas flights. These forecasts indicate the visibility of the atmo-sphere, the height of cloud layers, the tem-perature, and wind conditions at airports.

Marine forecasts of winds, visibility, and sea conditions are used by small boats and ships at sea and on the Great Lakes. Warnings of approaching storms are broadcast by radio stations, and warning flags are displayed in harbors and at Coast Guard stations. When hurricanes develop, small boats seek a safe

harbor, and larger ships avoid the path of these dangerous storms.

Tornadoes, blizzards, ice storms, and hur-ricanes are special weather conditions that endanger life and property. Warnings are issued when such storms are likely to occur. Hurricanes over warm, tropical waters are tracked by ship and aircraft reports and from satellite pictures. Frequent bulletins are issued to inform the public of the path of the storm, the wind velocity, and the high tides that occur as the storm moves toward shore.

Severe thunderstorms and tornadoes develop rapidly in spring and summer. These storms may produce winds up to 400 miles (644 kilometers) per hour. They can endanger life and do tremendous damage to property. Fore-casts and warnings are prepared to indicate where such storms are expected, and the public is advised to be on the alert by frequent bulletins from the National Weather Service.

C.B.J./M.K.H.

SEE ALSO: WEATHER, WEATHER MAP, WEATHER STATION

HURRICANE ANDREW
24 AUGUST 1992
5 AM EDT   926 MB

The massive, pinwheel hurricane cloud formation, as seen from a satellite (below) and by radar (left)

National Hurricane Center

NASA

© Tom Dietrich

Weather map Weather maps are used to show different weather conditions for any place in the world. Every minute of the day, WEATHER STATIONS, satellites, RADAR, and weather balloons are making detailed measurements and recordings of weather conditions such as temperature, wind direction, and AIR PRESSURE. This data is collected and fed into powerful super-computers that build a complete picture of weather conditions around the world. The most common type of weather map is called the *surface weather map.* Simplified versions of this type of map appear in newspapers and on television weather reports.

To save space and time, weather symbols have been designed to show the different kinds of weather. Most symbols look like the weather elements they represent. All countries of the world that make weather maps agree to use the same symbols. These symbols are a sign language that anyone can learn.

Each weather station is represented on a weather map by a small circle. This circle is left white if the sky is clear; it is made partly black if the sky is partly cloudy, and made completely black is the sky is covered by clouds. Placed around each circle are the weather symbols and figures to show the direction and speed of the wind, the temperature, the DEW POINT, the type of clouds, the air pressure, and change in pressure during the past three hours. The amount and type of precipitation is also shown.

To analyze the map, meteorologists draw lines that pass through the stations reporting the same air pressure. These lines, called *isobars*, define areas of high and low pressure over the map area. Winds tend to blow clockwise around high pressure areas, and counterclockwise around low pressure areas. In areas where there are big differences in air pressure, winds tend to be stronger. The closer together the isobars are, therefore, the more violent the weather is.

Further study of the map will show zones of important changes in weather, temperature, wind direction, and clouds. Such zones occur between air masses, and are called weather *fronts*. Various frontal symbols are used on the map to show the different kinds of fronts.

The final step is to identify the AIR MASSES. Air masses are large bodies of air sometimes 1,000 miles (1,600 kilometers) wide, which have uniform temperature and moisture conditions. Cold air masses are colder than the surface they are moving over, and usually originate over polar regions. Warm air masses are warmer than the surface they are moving over. Most warm air masses originate over tropical oceans and have a large supply of moisture.

The completed weather map gives a detailed picture of weather across the country. The map is compared with the past several maps showing observations made 12 to 24 hours before, to see what changes in weather are taking place and how the weather systems of high and low pressure are moving. By studying a sequence of maps, it is possible to make reliable weather forecasts one or two days in advance.　　　　　　　　　　　C.B.J./M.K.H.

SEE ALSO: WEATHER SERVICE, NATIONAL; WEATHER FORECASTING

Weather station To make an accurate weather forecast, *meteorologists* need millions of observations and measurements of atmospheric conditions from all over the world. One of the most important sources of this information is the weather station. Weather sta-

✳ **THINGS TO DO**

PREDICTING THE WEATHER FROM YOUR OWN STATION

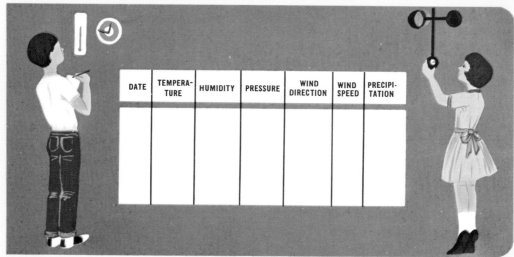

DATE	TEMPERA-TURE	HUMIDITY	PRESSURE	WIND DIRECTION	WIND SPEED	PRECIPI-TATION

1　To set up a weather station of your own you will need to construct instruments. Background information and instructions for making instruments are found in this encyclopedia under: **Anemometer, Barometer, Beaufort scale, Cloud, Convection, Evaporation, Fog, Frost, Hygrometer, Rain gauge, Precipitation, Snow gauge, Thermometer, Wind sock, Wind vane.**

2　Place the anemometer, rain gauge, and snow gauge in an open area away from buildings and trees.

3　Other instruments such as barometer, hygrometer and thermometer should be housed in shelter, free from the elements.

4　Prepare Beaufort scale and other charts from information gathered from the entries mentioned above, and keep with daily recording chart shown above.

5　Remember that these recordings are only approximate readings. Check with daily newspapers for comparisons.

tions are located in villages and cities, as well as on ships, on floating buoys, on tropical islands, and in the Arctic and Antarctic. Other facilities for collecting data include weather balloons, RADAR, and satellites.

Weather stations record weather conditions on land and at sea. There are thousands of permanent weather stations linked together by the World Meteorological Organization. Each station takes hourly measurements of wind speed and direction, temperature, AIR PRESSURE, humidity, precipitation (rainfall and snowfall), and other conditions. Reports from the individual stations are then sent by telephone every three hours to weather centers around the world.

WEATHER STATION INSTRUMENTS

Each weather station has a number of special instruments that record weather conditions. Wind direction and speed are measured using a WIND VANE and an ANEMOMETER, respectively. A wind vane, sometimes called a weather vane, is a device that turns freely on an upright rod and points in the direction from which the wind comes. An anemometer consists of several cups connected to a rod. When the wind blows, the cups turn. The stronger the winds blows, the faster the cups turn.

A THERMOMETER is used to measure the temperature of the air. Several different types of temperature measurements are made; the air temperature (called the *dry bulb* temperature), the wet bulb temperature (made using a thermometer that is not protected from the elements), and the maximum and minimum temperatures for the day. A continuous temperature record is made by a recording thermometer called a *thermograph*.

A BAROMETER is used to measure air pressure. Air pressure is closely related to weather and changes in air pressure can give a useful indication of weather to come.

The amount of MOISTURE, or HUMIDITY, in the air can be measured using a HYGROMETER. Humidity can also be found by calculating the difference between dry and wet temperature readings. The greater the difference between the temperatures of the dry and wet bulbs, the lower the humidity.

To measure rainfall and snowfall, weather stations use RAIN GAUGES. These gauges are cylinders that collect precipitation. The depth

Top: A weather station in Colorado
Middle: An anemometer, which measures wind speed
Bottom: A maximum/minimum thermometer

of rain or snow that has collected in the gauge indicates the amount of precipitation that has fallen.

WEATHER BALLOONS

In some weather stations, large weather balloons are sent aloft to measure conditions in the upper atmosphere. Each balloon carries an instrument called a RADIOSONDE, which makes and transmits measurements of temperature, pressure, and humidity in the atmosphere. Wind direction and speed can be calculated by tracking the movements of the balloon from the ground.

RADAR

Radar is used to measure precipitation in distant locations. A radar transmitter sends out radio waves, which are reflected by rain, snow, and ice particles in clouds. The reflection bounces back to the transmitter like an echo, and appears on a screen that is similar to a television screen. The amount of reflection indicates how heavily the rain or snow is falling and the distance the storm is from the transmitter.

Doppler radars, a new generation of weather radars based on the DOPPLER EFFECT, are being installed throughout the U.S. during the early- and mid-1990s. Unlike older systems, Doppler radars can measure the speed and direction of dust, snow, ice, and water particles inside storm systems. The devices are sensitive enough to measure gusts of seemingly clear air. The Doppler effect can be measured up to a distance of about 80 miles (130 km). Traditional measurements, made by both new and old generation radars, can be made reliably up to about 250 miles (400 km) from the transmitter.

WEATHER SATELLITES

Weather satellites constantly circle the earth, beaming back pictures of cloud and temperature patterns. Meteorologists use these pictures to spot hurricanes and other dangerous storms, and to plot storm movements.

There are two main types of weather satellites. *Geostationary satellites* orbit the earth about 22,300 miles (35,890 km) above the equator. The satellite moves in unison with

A meteorologist monitors signals from the Doppler NEXRAD (Next Generation Radar).

NOAA

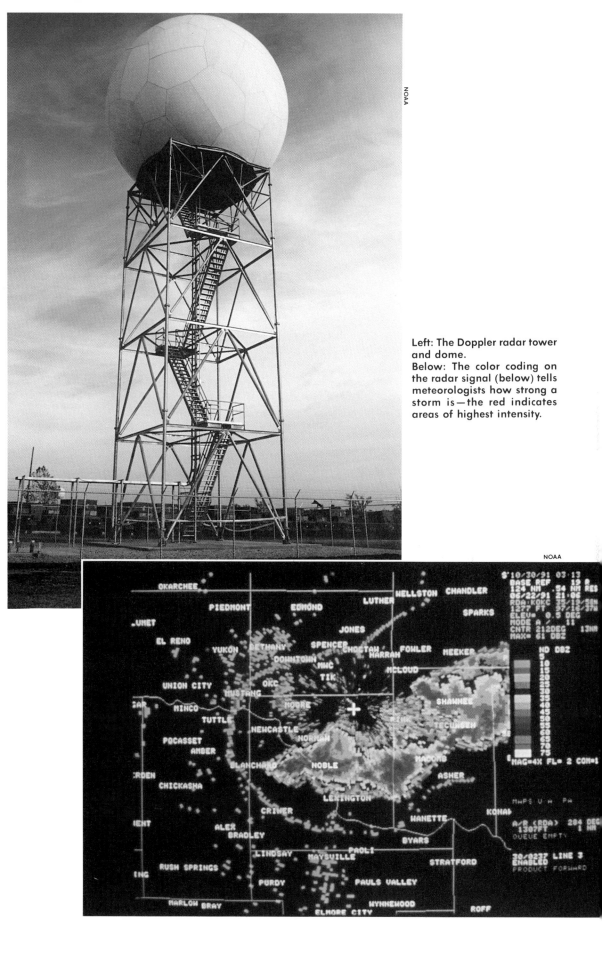

NOAA

Left: The Doppler radar tower and dome.
Below: The color coding on the radar signal (below) tells meteorologists how strong a storm is—the red indicates areas of highest intensity.

NOAA

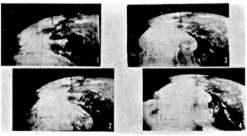

NASA

This series of photographs taken at an altitude of about 450 statute miles (724 kilometers) show a cloud mass lying over northeastern United States and Canada.

the earth's rotation so that it stays in one position over the earth. *Polar-orbiting satellites* circle the world from pole to pole. Their orbits are much lower than that of geostationary satellites—between 500 and 900 miles (805 and 1450 km) above the earth. Together the two types of satellites provide continuous detailed weather observations.   M.K.H.

SEE ALSO: SATELLITE, WEATHER FORECASTING; WEATHER MAP; WEATHER SERVICE, NATIONAL

Weather symbol see Weather forecasting, Weather map

Weather vane see Wind vane

Weathering Weathering is the chemical and physical change which occurs when rocks are exposed to weather. Soil is produced from rocks and minerals by the effects of air and water. It seems hard to believe that air can affect rock at all, but it is known that rock can be reduced to fine silt and sand in desert areas.

The main chemical change caused by air is *oxidation*. The oxygen in the air reacts with the minerals in a rock to form oxides, which are often loose and powdery. QUARTZ is about the only common mineral unaffected by air weathering. Feldspar and mica, two other common minerals in igneous rocks, contain aluminum, iron, and magnesium compounds. When these minerals are weathered, they form water soluble salts and clay. Further disintegration of the rock is caused by the abrasive, or wearing, effect of wind- and water-borne sand particles and pebbles. The weathering of most rocks is very slow; but weather can eventually remove entire mountain systems.

Water is very effective in mechanical weathering because it expands upon freezing. Water freezing in cracks in a rock can split off *(exfoliate)* pieces of the rock. D. A. B.

SEE ALSO: EROSION, GEOLOGY, OXIDATION

Web see Spiders

Wedge see Machines, simple

Weed A weed is any plant growing where it is not wanted and not useful. Many plants become weeds when they are introduced into new areas. Others are weeds when they crowd out crops in cultivated land.

Weed control Man has several reasons for wanting to control or rid his land of weeds. In the city, the homeowner finds weeds in his lawn unattractive. They use up the water and fertilizer which should be consumed by grass. On farmlands, weeds in fields of grain do the same damage. They crowd out the wanted plants. The yield-per-acre of a crop is greatly reduced in proportion to the quantity of weeds in the field.

Cultivated plants have difficulty existing without man's help. Delicate hybrids have lost some of the traits needed to exist when conditions are not too desirable for growth. Weeds, on the other hand, have always had to fend for themselves and are often able to exist under the most undesirable circumstances.

Man has employed various methods to remove wild plants. Weeds can be removed by pulling up or by plowing under. Careful selection of seeds is necessary to avoid buying a kind with large amounts of weed seeds in the mixture. Insects which are pests of weeds may be introduced into an area. Some planters promote the spread of a disease which attacks only particular weeds. Roadsides and areas along railroad tracks can be burned to clear the ground of weeds. Finally, many *herbicides,* chemicals that kill weeds, are available.

Maleic hydrozide, a herbicide, has the property of inhibiting plant growth. It causes cells to stop dividing. In small amounts, it is

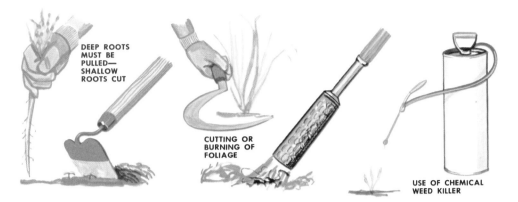

DEEP ROOTS MUST BE PULLED—SHALLOW ROOTS CUT

CUTTING OR BURNING OF FOLIAGE

USE OF CHEMICAL WEED KILLER

Controlling weeds is one way of changing the balance of nature.

useful in slowing down the formation of buds on fruit trees. In large quantities, it is used to kill such pests as quack grass and wild onion. Another herbicide is 2,4-D (2,4-dichloro-phenoxyacetic acid). This herbicide has a selective action. It will kill only certain plant life. A concentration of .1 percent of 2,4-D is sufficient. Another often used compound is 2,4,5-T (trichlorophenoxyacetic acid). It is effective in destroying such pests as poison ivy and Japanese honeysuckle.

A related problem is developing as man uses more and more herbicides. The toxic compounds are appearing in natural bodies of water. In cities, rain carries weed killers from lawns to sewers, which drain into lakes, rivers, or streams. Thus, man is polluting his water supply. Industrial plants that filter water for human consumption must detect and eliminate these new organic synthetics which are finding their way into ground and surface water sources.

Destroying wild plants or weeds rob many ground animals and birds of a potential food supply. Fruits and seeds of weeds may be the only food available. As these food sources are destroyed, wildlife is forced to move to new areas. Weeds also serve as a hiding place or nesting ground for smaller animals who need to avoid detection from their larger natural enemies. Thus, controlling weeds is another step by man toward upsetting the BALANCE OF NATURE with little concern for the consequence of his actions.   H. J. C.
SEE ALSO: HERB, WILD FLOWER

Weevil see Beetles, Plant pests

Weigela (wye-GEEL-uh) Weigela is a large, spreading shrub with branches that hang or droop over. It may reach 15 feet (4.6 meters). The leaves are simple and opposite on the branches. They are *deciduous,* meaning their leaves drop in fall.

The petals on the weigela flower form a bell or trumpet. They appear in spring or early summer. The flowers may be red, purple, or white. The fruit is a fleshy berry.

New hybrids are always being developed. They are collectively called *Weigela hybrida.* Some kinds have variegated leaves with white or yellow markings.

The weigela is native to Asia. It was named for C. Weigel, a Swiss doctor. It is a member of the HONEYSUCKLE or Caprifoliaceae family.   H. J. C.
SEE ALSO: SHRUB

Weighing machine see Balance

A common weigela   J. W. Thompson

※ **THINGS TO DO**

MAKING SCALES FOR WEIGHING MATERIALS

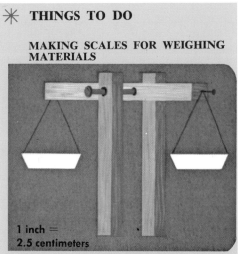

1 inch =
2.5 centimeters

Materials: pieces of wood about eighteen inches long, heavy wire, two metal pie pans, nut and bolt, drill with a bit slightly larger than the bolt diameter.

1 **Pattern your construction from the adjoining illustration. The wooden "T" should balance on the bolt between the two wooden uprights.**

2 **A variety of objects at the hardware store may be used as weights, such as nuts, plumber's bobs, curtain weights, and similar metal pieces. Weigh each one, and paint the ounces or pounds on it.**

3 **There are many times in experimenting when the recipe calls for different quantities of various chemicals. These may be weighed out rather accurately on your homemade scales.**

4 **Compare the weights of equal measurements of sugar, water, iron filings, mercury, flour, and cotton. Draw conclusions from your recordings.**

Weight The weight of any object is the force with which it is pulled toward the center of the earth. This force is directly related to the *mass* of the object. Mass is a basic characteristic of matter. It is also dependent on the distance of the object from the center of the earth.

The weight of an object is obtained by using a spring scale calibrated in units of weight. Ounces, pounds, and tons are weight units in the British system of units. Newtons and dynes are weight units in the metric system. The weight of an object can be obtained by multiplying the mass of an object by the acceleration due to gravity, *g*. On Earth the acceleration has the following standard value: 980.665 cm/sec^2 or 32.174 ft/sec^2.

The pull of the earth is called the *force of gravity.* It is slightly greater at the poles than at the equator. This is due to the fact that the earth is flatter at the poles than at the equator. The earth's surface is actually nearer its center at the poles. Therefore, an object of mass one kilogram would have a weight of 9.78 newtons at the equator. The same object would weigh 9.83 newtons at the poles.

Weight is greatest at the earth's surface. The weight of a body decreases as the body goes up from the surface. Weight also decreases as the body goes below the earth's surface. At some point above the earth's surface, the force of the earth's attraction approaches zero. At this point the object is said to be *weightless.*   A.J.H./H.W.M.

SEE ALSO: GRAVITY, MASS, MEASUREMENT, WEIGHTLESSNESS

Weight arm see Machines, simple

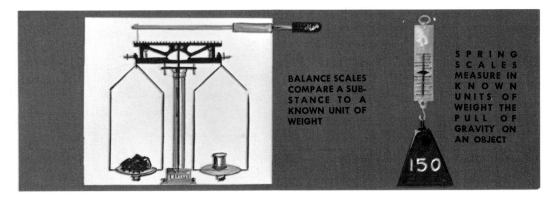

BALANCE SCALES COMPARE A SUBSTANCE TO A KNOWN UNIT OF WEIGHT

SPRING SCALES MEASURE IN KNOWN UNITS OF WEIGHT THE PULL OF GRAVITY ON AN OBJECT

150

Weightlessness Weightlessness, or zero-g, is demonstrated by a body falling in a vacuum such as outer space. No resistance is offered to the body as its mass attempts to follow the gravitational pull of Earth. If resistance, or support, is measured by placing the body on a scale, its "weight" is measured. If no resistance or support is offered, and the body falls freely, it no longer has any weight. Bodies in orbit, such as the moon, the Earth or a space ship, fall freely. The moon falls in the Earth's gravitational field, and the Earth in the sun's. All the nine known planets fall into the sun's gravitational field.

What causes an object on Earth or the moon to have weight is the comparatively large mass of these bodies. A space ship does not have such a mass and therefore does not noticeably affect the bodies within its confines, which fall freely together with the space ship, and hence are relatively weightless.

Weightlessness poses many problems to people as they travel and work in space. Because ordinary food and water would float about the cabin of a spacecraft, food for space flights must be prepared in special ways. It can be prepared in a puree form and packaged in squeeze tubes, dehydrated or powdered and stored in plastic bags, or served in solid bite-sized chunks packaged in edible wrappers. Water is most often packaged in squeeze tubes.

Because of zero gravity, special tools have been developed to allow people to work in space. Electrical and magnetic devices have been developed to temporarily hold an astronaut to the outside of a spacecraft. These devices have been successfully used by astronauts during their thrilling "space walks."

Skylab flights have proven that humans can tolerate a prolonged state of weightlessness, provided their environment is engineered with this condition in mind, to avoid discomfort in many daily functions.

K.A.E.

SEE ALSO: SPACE MEDICINE, SPACE STATION, SPACE TRAVEL, SPACE VEHICLE

August Weismann

Weismann, August (VYS-mahn, OW-goost) (1834-1914) August Weismann was a German biologist who originated the theory of the continuity of germ plasm. In his germ-plasm theory, he proposed that living organisms contain a special substance (the germ plasm) which, unlike the body of the organism, does not perish, but is transferred from generation to generation. Germ plasm is formed by, and takes the properties of, germ plasm which already exists.

Weismann declared that the germ plasm governs every part of the organism, and cannot be changed by environmental forces. He also believed that the hereditary substances from the two parents are blended in the fertilized egg. He said that a form of nuclear division must take place, at this time each new nucleus receives only half the germ plasm contained in the original nucleus. Weismann's theory was proved correct and he later was able to theorize, with the help of other biologists, that the germ plasm was located in what are now called the CHROMOSOMES of the egg or sperm nuclei. This theory became the basis of much of the modern science of *genetics*.

Weismann was born in Frankfurt-am-Main on January 17, 1834. He studied medicine at the University of Göttingen from 1852 until 1856. After working under an outstanding biologist in Giessen for a few years, he became Professor of Zoology at the University of Freiburg. There he remained until his retirement in 1912.   D. H. J.

SEE ALSO: EMBRYOLOGY

Welding   see Arc, Engineering

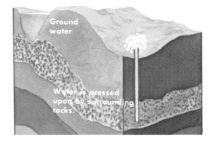

Well A well is an opening in the earth, which may be drilled or dug to reach water that collects underground. This collection of water is called *water table.*

The water may exist in pore spaces between rock fragments or in fractures within the rock. After a hole has been drilled through the rock, a pipe is lowered to reach the water. A pump is then installed at the surface to supply the power needed to lift the water up through the pipe. A pump may be operated by hand or by some other mechanical means. Because of *pressure,* a hand pump only works to a depth of 32 feet (9.8 meters).

When the underground water seeps into a basin-like reservoir where hard rock layers press upon it, the water will escape or forcibly flow when the underground reservoir is tapped. This is called *hydrostatic pressure* and no other power is needed to bring the water to the surface. This is an *artesian well.*

The name "artesian" comes from the Artois region in northern France where natural artesian wells were observed in Roman times. Today the term "artesian well" is generally applied to a well that has been drilled into any underground basin of water that is under pressure from the enclosing rock.

Water collects in a basin-like underground cavity where rock layers press upon it. This water, when tapped by a well pipe, will flow up without any other energy being needed. Such self-flowing water sources are artesian wells.

The water from an artesian well is likely to be pure because it has been filtered through sand and semiporous rocks. Such a well may tap a source of water in a region that is otherwise very dry, such as the Sahara Desert or the interior of Australia. In these places, artesian wells make crop irrigation possible.

Because some artesian wells go down as far as 5,000 feet (1,524 meters), their water temperature gives scientists a clue to the interior heat of the earth.   D.A.B.

SEE ALSO: WATER TABLE

Weller, Thomas H. (1915-   ) Weller is a U.S. bacteriologist and virologist who shared in the 1954 NOBEL PRIZE in physiology and medicine for research in tissue culture techniques. This work led to the eventual development of a vaccine for polio.

Dr. Weller, working with Doctors Enders and Robbins, succeeded in developing a technique for growing and identifying poliomyelitis virus in living non-nerve tissue. Dr. Weller also studied the causative agents of chicken pox and mumps.   P.P.S.

Werner, Alfred (1866-1919) Werner Alfred earned the 1913 NOBEL PRIZE in chemistry for his studies of how atoms link up in molecules. This was an important contribution to inorganic chemistry.

Alfred Werner developed a coordination theory of valence. This led to a means of classifying inorganic compounds. Werner studied the arrangements of atoms in complex inorganic molecules and investigated the stereochemistry of cobalt, chromium, and platinum. His work contributed to the definition and understanding of *isomers.*

A.J.H.

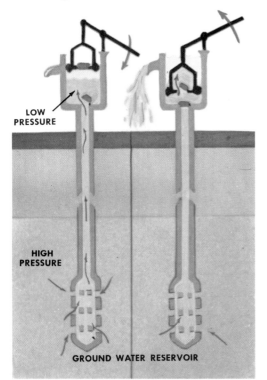

LOW PRESSURE

HIGH PRESSURE

GROUND WATER RESERVOIR

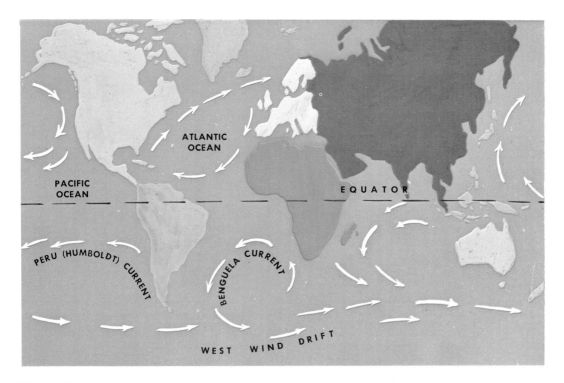

ATLANTIC
OCEAN

PACIFIC
OCEAN

E Q U A T O R

PERU (HUMBOLDT) CURRENT

BENGUELA CURRENT

WEST WIND DRIFT

West Wind Drift Around the Antarctic (South) Pole blow some of the coldest, bleakest winds on earth. These winds blow from west to east. Because their latitude is approximately 40° south, they have been named the "Roaring Forties."

As these winds circle the pole, they drive the ocean in a perpetual eastward drift of cold water. This current is called the "West Wind Drift." As the drift encounters the southern tip of South America, part of it is sheared off to travel up the west coast as the Peru (Humboldt) Current. A similar action at the tip of Africa produces the Benguela Current, which travels along its west coast. R. N. J.

SEE ALSO: CURRENTS, OCEAN

Westerlies The westerlies are wind belts found in both hemispheres. The full name for this wind belt is *prevailing westerlies*. The term prevailing indicates that the winds of this belt blow from the southwest most of the time.

The winds of the prevailing westerlies originate in the high-pressure belts of the HORSE LATITUDES and blow towards the poles as far as the subpolar lows. As they move toward the poles, they are deflected by the earth's rotation. They become southwesterlies in the Northern Hemisphere and northwesterlies in the Southern Hemisphere. Unlike the steady trade winds, the winds of the prevailing westerlies vary greatly in both strength and direction. This creates a belt of ever-changing weather conditions, especially in the Northern Hemisphere. A series of high and low pressure centers develop in this region and move in a general west-to-east direction.

The strength of the westerlies increases with latitude. Their strength is also greater over the uninterrupted surface of the ocean than over the land. H. S. G.

SEE ALSO: WEATHER

Wet bulb see Hygrometer

Wet cell see Battery

Wetting agent A wetting agent reduces SURFACE TENSION where a liquid meets a solid surface, causing the liquid to spread more easily and be more easily absorbed. Wetting agents are widely used as DETERGENTS and in the textile industry.

RIGHT WHALE

FINBACK WHALE

GRAY WHALE

THESE ARE BALEEN WHALES

Whale A whale is a true mammal. Baby whales are called *calves,* and are fed milk from their mother's bodies. Most whales have hair in the form of scattered bristles. Whales breathe air; they come to the surface about every twenty minutes. Some whales have stayed under water for an hour. After surfacing, whales breathe out air from their lungs through a blow-hole on top of their heads. This blast of warm air vaporizes when it reaches the colder surface air, and looks like a spout of water. Thick layers of fat, called *blubber,* protect whales' bodies from the cold ocean waters. Whales are hunted for the oil found in their blubber.

Even though a whale has lungs, it must stay in water. The buoyancy of water supports its huge body. Otherwise, its tremendous weight would crush its lungs and bones. Whales have very acute hearing, even though the exterior ear opening is only the width of a pencil. The eye is also small. A 70-foot (21-meter) whale has an eyeball that is only about 5 inches (13 centimeters) in diameter.

There are about one hundred kinds of whales. They belong to the order of Cetaceans along with DOLPHINS and PORPOISES. True whales are divided into two groups—*baleen* and *toothed* whales. Baleen whales do not have teeth. Instead, many sheets, or plates, of thin, horn-like material, called *baleen,* hang from the roof of their mouths. As this whale swims open-mouthed through water, the fringed edges of baleen trap tiny fish and crustaceans, the only food whales eat. Water is ejected by pressing the tongue against the baleen.

Some *blue whales* (or sulfur-bottoms) are more than 100 feet (30 meters) long, thus making them the largest animals ever to have lived. The *right whales* were so named by whalers because they were the "right

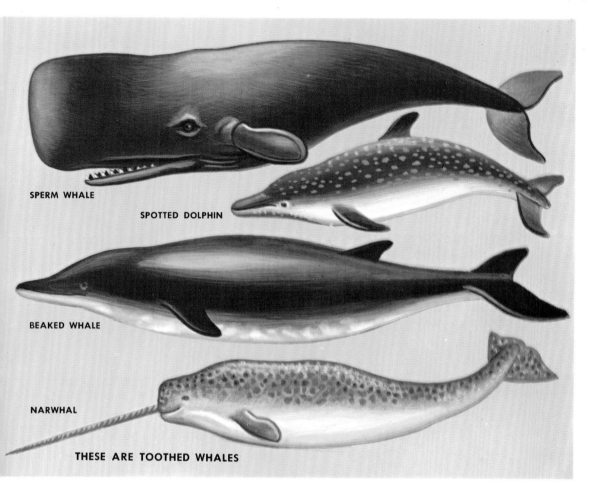

SPERM WHALE

SPOTTED DOLPHIN

BEAKED WHALE

NARWHAL

THESE ARE TOOTHED WHALES

whales to hunt.'' They offered little resistance, and were found closer to shore. They have been protected since 1935.

The *sperm whale* is the most distinguished of the toothed whale group. This is the ''Moby Dick'' of literary fame. The upper jaw is toothless but has pits into which the teeth of the lower jaw fit. The large head contains sperm oil and *spermaceti* for which this beast is hunted. Despite the tremendous size of many whales, only the sperm whale has a throat large enough to swallow a man. Enraged sperm whales have rammed and sunk whaling ships and have attacked men in water. Their average length is 60 feet (18 meters). They can swim at a depth of 5,000 feet (1,520 meters). Food consists of squid and cuttlefish. *Ambergris,* a rare substance formed in the sperm's stomach as a result of indigestion, is the base for some drugs and perfumes.

Except for hunters the whale has almost no natural enemies. Yet many whales are on the endangered species list. They include the blue, bowhead, finback, gray, humpback, sperm, and right whales. In 1946, the International Whaling Commission was organized to set up regulations and quotas on whaling. Only Russia, Japan, and Norway are still hunting whales for oil, blubber, and meat. Since the decrease in numbers of the large whales (there are only about 600 blue whales left) hunters kill smaller species or the young of large varieties. Helicopters spot a group, then ships are guided in for the kill. Boats also use sonar to locate them. After the whale has been harpooned, air is shot into it, causing it to float for easy transporting.

Whales must be protected, for it takes decades to replenish just a few. A blue whale mother gives birth to a single calf every two years. The calf will nurse for at least seven months before it can feed on its own. By this time it will measure over 50 feet (15 meters) long.   J.A.D./H.J.C.

SEE ALSO: CETACEA, INTERNATIONAL CONTROL OF NATURAL RESOURCES, MAMMALIA

Winter wheat is almost full grown when fields are plowed for the summer

Wheat harvesting in the Far West

Wheat Wheat is an annual plant of the GRASS family, one of the major CEREAL GRAINS of the world. It has been grown for over 6000 years. It grows best in fairly dry, temperate regions without much humidity.

The plant averages 3 feet (.9 meter) high. The leaves are long with linear venation. The stem is hollow except at the nodes. The flower head is an inflorescence with an average of 18 spikelets, each having from one to several flowers. The root system of the plant is fibrous and shallow.

The wheat grain, or FRUIT, is classified as *caryopsis*. The embryo and endosperm are surrounded by the *husk* or *bran* which is the fruit wall. *Graham flour* is the total grain crushed. *Whole wheat* has part of the bran removed, while *white flour* has it all out. *"Patent" flour* has the bran, embryo and aleurone layer removed. The finest is "angel food" which is only about 40% endosperm.

Durem wheat is hard, has red grain high in protein gluten and is used for spaghetti. More of the common soft wheats which have more starch are used for bakery goods. Spelt and Emmer wheats are hardy ancient varieties. Club and Polish wheats have limited cultivation in the United States. H. J. C.

Wheel and axle see Machines, simple

Whelk Whelks are large ocean snails with beautiful, coiled shells. The shell is like a suit of armor. It protects the soft, fleshy body inside the shell. Whelks belong to a large group of soft-bodied animals called *mollusks*.

When moving or eating, whelks push out a foot and head from the bottom of the shell. Like most snails, they plow slowly through the sand on this wide, muscular foot. The head, just in front of the foot, has a mouth and a pair of tentacles with eyes. When disturbed, whelks withdraw into the shell. A hard plate covering the bottom of the foot acts as a door to seal the opening.

This carnivorous snail competes with people for oysters and clams. They extend a *radula,* or tongue-like organ, from the mouth. By drilling holes through the mollusk shells, they are able to remove the flesh.

Female whelks may lay 1,500 eggs at one time. The young, born in protective cases, do not hatch until they have matured into young snails. Adults may reach a length of 9 inches (23 centimeters). E.P.L.

SEE ALSO: MOLLUSCA, SNAIL

The whelk lives below the tide line

Parts of a wheat grain

Whippoorwill

Whippoorwill The whippoorwill is a bird with a wide head, a wide, bristled mouth and a small, hooked bill. It calls its name tirelessly after sunset.

Although easy to hear, this bird, which is about the size of a robin, is very hard to see. Its barred brown plumage blends perfectly with the leaves. The whippoorwill prefers meadows near water and thick woods. It flies little except when searching out the beetles, moths and other insects that it likes. Then its flight is erratic. Its soft feathers make its flight soundless.

It builds no nest, simply laying its eggs in an unprotected depression in the leaves on the ground.

It is a member of the *goatsucker* family and is related to the nighthawk. It is common in the eastern United States. Similar birds, the *chuckwill's widow,* a larger bird, and *poorwill,* a smaller bird, are common in the South and Southwest, respectively.   E. R. B.

Whirlpool A whirlpool is a violently revolving current of water. It is caused by two currents or tides meeting, by the wind blowing against a tide, by irregular conditions on the bottom, or by certain shore formations.

As the water spins, it forms a low-pressure center into which floating objects are

A whirlpool in the ocean

drawn. Whirlpools form in oceans, lakes, and rivers. Famous whirlpools are the Maelstrom near Norway and Charybdis near Sicily. Though the powers of these two whirlpools are exaggerated, they are famous in legend and myth. The term "maelstrom" is another name for whirlpool.   D. A. B.

Whirlybird see Helicopter

White damp White damp is a term usually applied to *carbon monoxide* when it occurs as a poisonous gas in coal mines.

SEE: CARBON MONOXIDE, GAS

White light White light is made up of all colors. By shining white light through a prism, the various, combined colors can be broken into a rainbow-colored band called the spectrum.

SEE: COLOR, DISPERSION, LIGHT, PRISM, SPECTRUM

White mice The white mouse is a rodent. When full grown it is only 3 inches (7.6 centimeters) long, excluding its 2-inch (5-centimeter) tail. This white-furred, tamed mouse is often used in laboratory experiments. It is also an attractive house pet.

Scientists use white mice in great numbers. Biologists use them to study principles of heredity and the nature of certain diseases such as cancer; psychologists use them in studies of learning; and physiologists use them in determining the properties of medicines. Mice are often chosen for experiments in preference to other animals for several reasons. They are small, and thus require little living space and food. Because they are mammals, their bodies are similar to other domestic mammals and man. Because from five to eight baby mice are born at a time, in only three weeks after the parents mate, they make inexpensive laboratory animals. One disadvantage is that they are short-lived, becoming old near their third year.

The term white mouse is really a general name for several varieties which are hereditary types of *albinos*. Hobbyists, and other mouse fanciers, raise a part-white variety,

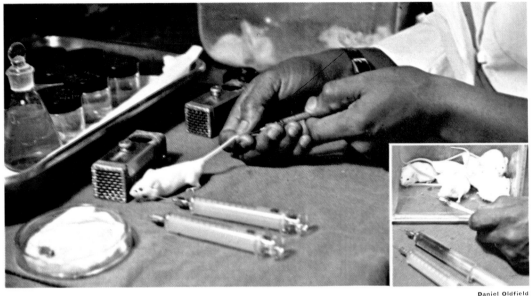

Daniel Oldfield

White mice are being used in laboratories to test cancer-stopping serums

a type with white fur but black eyes. There are also fancy fur varieties, such as those with bands of various-colored spots on the otherwise white fur. Then there are mouse varieties with solid coat colors such as chocolate, cream, and black fur. By breeding several of these varieties over several generations, one can finally breed offspring with a gray, mottled color *(agouti)* originally found in the wild variety of house mouse.

When white mice are kept as pets, food and water must always be kept in the cage because mice are so small they quickly starve and die of thirst. Since mice are small and quick-moving, they are best housed in a deep dry aquarium or in special cages. These tiny animals lose heat rapidly, and thus nesting material, such as wool yarn or shredded paper, should be provided.

White mice tend to be gentle if handled carefully, though young mice will nip at the caretaker's fingers. They can be tamed best by frequent, gentle handling that is started when the animals are about three weeks old.

As the young mice reach adulthood, they can be taught simple behaviors. They can learn to run through homemade box mazes and to operate wire exercise wheels. Psychologists have learned certain laws of mental behavior from experiments with white mice operating such devices.   D. A. B.

SEE ALSO: ALBINO, RODENTIA

White wax see Paraffin

Whitefish The whitefish is found in the Great Lakes. Average weight is about 5 pounds (2.25 kilograms), although some whitefish weigh as much as 20 pounds (9 kilograms). The whitefish is important because it is widely used as food.

The whitefish has its mouth on the underside of the head. It eats crustaceans and mollusks from the lake bottom. In spring it migrates to shallow waters to eat mosquito larvae; in summer it occupies deep water; in the autumn it again goes to shores to spawn. Many of the young are eaten by enemies, and thus lakes must be restocked each year. Gill nets are used to catch whitefish.   D. J. I.

SEE ALSO: PISCES

Erie whitefish from the Great Lakes
Chicago Natural History Museum

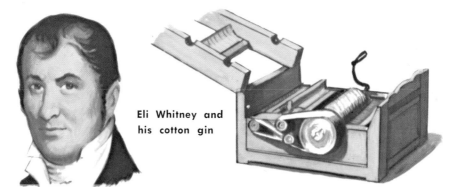

Eli Whitney and his cotton gin

Whitney, Eli (1765-1825) Eli Whitney invented the cotton gin, a machine to separate the lint from the seeds of the cotton. This was a simple, hand separated machine, but it could clean 50 pounds (23 kilograms) of lint a day. Its wooden cylinder was covered with rows of slender spikes. These spikes extended through a grid that was so fine that the cotton seeds could not pass through, although the lint could.

When Eli Whitney graduated from Yale College in 1792, he went to Georgia. While there he learned of the need for a machine that would separate cotton. Within three weeks he made a model of the cotton gin and was granted a patent on March 14, 1794.

With Phineas Miller, Whitney formed a partnership to manufacture his new machine in New Haven, Connecticut. Then on May 12, 1796, a patent for a slightly different cotton gin was granted to Hogden Holmes. Whitney took the matter to court, winning the battle in 1807. He was so embittered by the experience he gave up the manufacture of gins and began to manufacture fire arms at Whitneyville, Connecticut. By making guns with replaceable parts, he earned government contracts and became wealthy.

Whitney's most important contribution to manufacturing was the making of parts that could be interchanged, and of having different men make different parts. Thus Whitney pioneered in mass production.   D. H. J.

Whooping cough (HOO-ping) Whooping cough is a childhood disease. It is an inflammation of the breathing passages in the body and can be serious.

The germs causing whooping cough are called *Bordetella pertussis;* whooping cough is medically known as *pertussis.* The infection usually spreads from a patient in the early stages of the disease to a susceptible child—one who has not been immunized or is not immune from already having had the disease. Pertussis vaccine is quite effective in giving immunity. The germs are carried by minute droplets expelled into the surrounding air during coughs. Once these germs are inhaled, they lodge in the respiratory membranes of the throat and lungs. Here they multiply rapidly for a week or more—the incubation period.

At first symptoms of an ordinary cold appear. The nose runs and mucus comes up from the throat. The sick person begins to cough, mostly at night. These symptoms indicate the beginning of the most contagious period. The coughing spells become more frequent, last longer, and are more severe. Eyes tear during prolonged coughs.

After about two weeks, there develop severe and explosive fits of rapid coughing followed by the "whoop" as deep breaths are desperately sucked in. During this period the violent coughing may cause vomiting. Then, gradually, if no complications set in, the attacks become less frequent and less severe. The disease usually lasts about six weeks.

It is extremely important that children be immunized against pertussis by a triple Diphtheria-Pertussis-Tetanus (DPT) injection at two, four, and six months of age, with a booster shot ten to twelve months later. The pertussis vaccine often causes a fever, and occasionally a convulsion, in a susceptible infant, so that parents sometimes do not wish to bring their child back for the second one. However, at least three shots are needed to provide immunity; four are preferable. Children who develop pertussis are usually hospitalized, isolated, and treated with antibiotics. In a very ill child, hyperimmune globulin (a specific anti-pertussis globulin) might be tried.   D.L.D./E.S.S.

Whooping crane see Crane

Courtesy Society For Visual Education, Inc.

Wild goldenrod is often considered undesirable

Wild flower Any flowering plant which is not deliberately planted and cultivated by man is considered a wild flower. Often, such plants are called weeds. Whether a plant is wild depends upon the country and condition under which it is growing. The *dandelion* and *goldenrod* are considered wild flowers and pesky weeds in the United States. However, in some countries these plants are grown in gardens. Wild flowers grow and spread their seeds in fields, roadsides, and wastelands, often crowding out plants we want to grow.

The name given to a wild plant varies with the locality. Its common name depends upon the region in which it appears. The only true way to identify a wild flower is by its genus and species. For example, *evening primrose, sun cups,* and *golden eggs* are all names for the same plant. Its true scientific name is *Oenothera ovata.* The use of the latter name can be recognized by botanists in any country in the world.

There are more than 25,000 kinds of wild flowers currently identified in North America. Hundreds are classified in every plant family. Often, wild flowers are grouped together according to the seasons of the year in which the flower appears. *Trillium, merrybells,* and *jack-in-the-pulpit* are spring flowers. *Cinquefoil, geranium,* and *bluebell* bloom in summer, while *goldenrod, chicory,* and *New England aster* are fall flowers.

Other wild flowers may be grouped together by their locality or environment. *Asters, shooting star,* and *mullein* are prairie flowers. *Skunk cabbage, marsh marigold,* and *swamp rose* grow well in bogs. *Spring beauty, dogtooth violet,* and *heartleaf-lily* are found in woods. *Sand verbena, gold poppy,* and *cactus* are desert plants. *Water hyacinth, pond lily,* and *bladderwort* thrive in water.

Wild flowers may be compared to wild animals, for both live under the law of survival of the fittest. Since they are not protected by man, only the strong ones survive. They adapt to their rugged existence. When a particular trait which improves its ability to live in adverse conditions appears in a species by mutation, plants having that trait will thrive and reproduce successfully. Soon, these characteristics appear in most of the plants. The constant improvement of weed-killing chemicals, for example, is producing wild flowers capable of withstanding spraying treatment.

Wild flowers have an extensive and sturdy root system. Since most of their aboveground parts die in the winter, the roots or underground stems are the beginnings of a new year's crop the following spring. The seeds that wild flowers produce also ensure the continuation of the species.

Wild flowers have unusual systems of seed and fruit dispersal. Many seeds are "hitchhikers" that attach themselves to any moving organism brushing by them. Other seeds depend upon wind or water dispersal. The fleshy fruit of some wild flowers are picked and eaten by birds, who then drop the seeds far from the original mother plant.

Most wild plants cannot be grown as casually and easily as cultivated varieties. The situation is similar to trying to place wild animals in captivity, expecting them to adjust and reproduce in a strange environment. Wild plants need special kinds of soils, temperatures, and light conditions. The extensive root systems also make wild flowers difficult to transplant.

Wild flowers are most significant in a community of living things. They are among the first plants to appear in an area destroyed by fire, flood, or erosion. In the succession of plant life in an area, wild flowers have a vital niche in the balance of nature.

DISAPPEARANCE OF WILD FLOWERS

Many wild flowers are rapidly disappearing in the United States. As man takes more and more unused land for towns, cities, farms, and highways, he destroys the breeding grounds for the wild flowers. Nature also takes its toll. Fires, erosions, floods, volcanic erup-

MAKING A WILD FLOWER COLLECTION

1. Gather specimen, flower and leaf. (See pgs. 1872 and 1873 for some help in identification.) Care should be taken not to pull up or otherwise destroy valuable plants.
2. Press flower between newspapers, which will absorb moisture.
3. Change papers daily until specimens are dry. A plant press or weights on top will help smooth them out.
4. Mount specimens on paper or cardboard, using transparent tape.
5. Label each with its plant name, habitat, place collected, and date of collection.

tions, and dust storms eliminate whole sections of these herbs.

Frequently the beauty of a species of wild flower contributes to its own extermination. The *lady's slipper,* which has several species in many parts of the United States, is a curious and lovely species of the orchid family. At one time it flourished in large numbers in the hilly sections of the eastern states. Now careless picking of the flower has made it a rare plant.

Every section of the country has flowers which have been almost exterminated. The collector who happens to find a rare wild flower should admire it where he finds it and not pick it or dig it up. Such a careful attitude will preserve these flowers for future generations to admire.

Many organizations are concerned about the survival of wild flowers. Preservation societies have established wild flower sanctuaries. State governments have passed legislation making it illegal to destroy certain wild flowers. People who randomly pick a species that is becoming extinct can be fined. Commercial florists and nurseries sell wild flower seeds in an effort to help preserve some of the beautiful garden species.

The United States Fish and Wildlife Service in Washington, D.C., has lists of plants that should be protected in different sections of North America. It will cooperate with individuals or groups who want to save and restore flowers which have become, or are becoming, extinct.

The illustrations on pages 1872-73 show some of the lovely wild flowers found in the United States.　　　　　　　H. J. C.
SEE ALSO: PLANTS, CLASSIFICATION OF; PLANTS, INSECTIVOROUS; PLANTS, SUCCULENT; PLANTS, MEDICINAL

Wildcat see Cat family

Wildebeest see Gnu

Wilderness A wilderness is a community of plants and animals in a region where people usually do not live. It is a fragile, unique area, easily damaged by human habitation.

There are very few wilderness areas left in the United States. Canada wisely began preserving wildlife areas in 1885, when a small tract of land was set aside for the people. It now has a national park system that includes 50,000 square miles (129,500 square kilometers). In 1964, the U.S. Congress set up the National Wilderness Preservation System, which reserved over 9 million acres (3.5 million hectares) as wilderness areas. The Council on Environmental Quality is struggling to preserve entire natural communities for endangered species. Still, air and water pollution endanger wilderness areas. Saving them is complex and demanding. It requires regional, national, and international awareness and action.

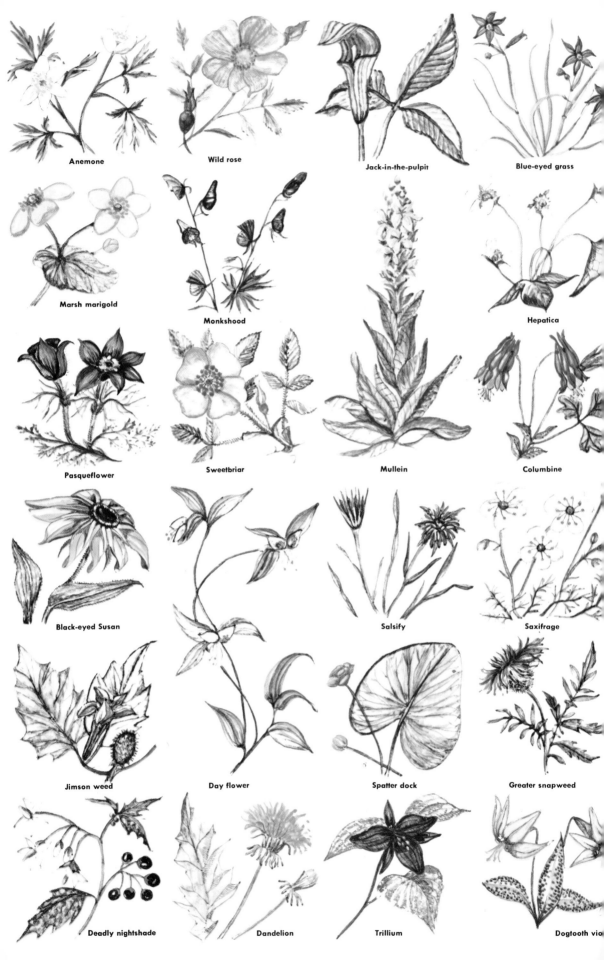

Anemone

Wild rose

Jack-in-the-pulpit

Blue-eyed grass

Marsh marigold

Monkshood

Hepatica

Pasqueflower

Sweetbriar

Mullein

Columbine

Black-eyed Susan

Salsify

Saxifrage

Jimson weed

Day flower

Spatter dock

Greater snapweed

Deadly nightshade

Dandelion

Trillium

Dogtooth vio

Adder's tongue fern

Skunk cabbage

Dutchman's breeches

Moccasin flower

Gentian

Smilax

Queen Anne's Lace

Blue bottle

Pokeweed

Milkweed

Goldenrod

Indian paintbrush

Bluets

Resurrection plant

Jacob's ladder

Blue bonnet

Heath-spotted orchis

Yellow lily

May apple

Sand verbena

Phlox

Solomon's seal

Some progress has been made. In 1973, the U.S. National Parks Service established its policies for the next 100 years. Wilderness areas are to be protected by buffer zones. Human residence is to be kept at a minimum. Only a limited number of hikers will be able to explore wilderness areas. Cabins, trailer parks, and other accomodations will be phased out or moved.

The wilderness area in Alaska was recently reduced when the oil industry laid 789 miles (1,270 kilometers) of pipeline. This fragile arctic ecosystem is now in danger of water pollution, oil spills, and erosion of the tundra.

Africa has the greatest areas of wilderness lands. Conservationists are concerned because hunters and poachers have moved into these remote areas.　　　　H.J.C.

SEE ALSO: BALANCE OF NATURE, INTERNATIONAL CONTROL OF NATURAL RESOURCES

Willet The willet is a long-legged wading bird of North America recognized by its whistling cry and black-and-white wing pattern.

Willow There are many varieties of willow trees and shrubs. The willow family (Salicaceae) includes cottonwood and poplar. The leaves of the common willow trees are long, thin, and pointed. The branches and twigs bend easily and are yellow even in winter. A twig will root in water.

Willows are among the earliest trees to get their leaves in spring after the *catkins*. Since ancient times, the willow has served in many ways; the branches for basket weaving, the wood for charcoal making, *salicin* (a substance in the bark) for medicines, and tannic acid for tanning. Weeping willow and yellow willow are decorative garden trees.

Willows generally are found in the Northern Hemisphere; a few are found in the tropics. Some, only inches high, grow near the Arctic Circle.　　　　C.L.K.

Wilson, Charles Thomson Rees (1869-1959) Charles Wilson shared the 1927 NOBEL PRIZE in physics with

✳ **THINGS TO DO**

MAKING A WIND SOCK

1　Sew a piece of cotton mesh or light weight cloth in the shape of a cone.
2　Tack the wide mouth of the cone to a stiff wire circle.
3　Nail a dowel rod to a wooden base for the support. With string tie the cone on the upper end of the rod.
4　Use a compass to determine exact direction. Paint N, S, E, and W on the base of the support when you have it in its permanent setting.

ARTHUR COMPTON. He invented the Wilson cloud chamber, a devise used to study subatomic particles.

Wilson was a particle physicist. He studied the condensation of tiny droplets of water in the absence of dust; ions (charged particles); and atmospheric electricity. His cloud chamber used ionized gases as condensation nuclei. This made it possible to detect subatomic particles, such as alpha and beta particles.　　　　A.J.H.

Wind When air moves along the surface of the earth it is called wind. A wind is really a huge *convection* current, consisting of sinking cool air and rising warm air. Some of these currents extend only a few miles, others cover thousands of miles.

SEE: AIR MASSES, CYCLONE, TORNADO, WEATHER

Wind sock At an airport, a wind sock serves as a very large and plainly visible indicator of wind direction for pilots. A pilot must know the direction of the wind. This simple weather instrument is necessary particularly at small local airports where there is no radio system to advise the pilot of the wind direction.

The wind sock is made of a netted material, which will catch wind but allow it to flow through. It is open and large at one end, and tapers gradually to a pointed closed end. It is usually anywhere from 3 to 6 feet (.9 to 1.8 meters) long. It is white or brightly colored so that it is easily visible.

Airplanes take off and land against the wind. Since the wind sock is large and placed in a position that is easily visible to the pilot, it assists him in determining the direction in which he will take off or land.

The wind sock also helps to determine the speed of the wind, because it goes limp in light winds and straightens out in strong breezes. V.V.N.

Wind tunnel A wind tunnel is a chamber in which a model aircraft is supported. An airstream of known force is blown through the chamber. Recording gauges report how the model reacts. From this information designers determine how the actual plane will respond in flight.

Wind vane The familiar "weather vane" is really a wind vane. It shows the direction from which the wind is blowing. This weather instrument points into the wind or to windward. For example, a wind vane that is

pointing south shows a south wind.

The wind vane has a broad tail which offers greater resistance to the wind than the narrow arrow-shaped end. A wind from the south will swing the tail of the vane toward the north, thus causing the arrow-shaped end to point to the south.

At most weather stations, the wind vane is connected to an electrical indicator on the compass dial. The indicator displays the wind direction inside the office of the station, making it more convenient to read and record the wind direction frequently.

Although this instrument is considered relatively simple in structure, it is really very important. Wind directions help foretell the WEATHER. V. V. N.

SEE ALSO: WEATHER STATION

✳ **THINGS TO DO**

WHICH WAY IS THE WIND BLOWING?

1 inch = 2.5 centimeters

1 Saw an arrow out of a piece of wood an inch thick. Hammer a long spike from the top edge center through to the underside. The nail should protrude two inches.

2 Drill a hole in one end of a thick dowel rod. Fasten the dowel upright to a wooden base or it may be driven directly into the ground near your weather station.

3 Oil the hole in the dowel before setting the arrow onto the stand. This will reduce friction as the wind vane turns with the breeze.

U.S. Department of Agriculture photo

A dense growth of chokecherries serves as a windbreak.

Charles B. Johnson

A simple windlass can be used to hold a rotating water wheel in place

Windbreak A windbreak, sometimes called a *tree shelter belt,* is a device used to help prevent dust storms. The trees break the force of the prevailing westerly winds. A great shelter belt was planned and begun in 1936 for the great plains area of the United States. It extends from Texas to North Dakota. Today it includes row upon row of trees. This was a cooperative effort on the part of farmers and the federal government.

The use of trees as a windbreak is not a new idea. Many farms on the plains had their own windbreaks long before 1937. These windbreaks are not only used over large general areas, but they are also locally used by farmers to protect certain areas of their property which are vulnerable to high winds. Usually plowed fields and hillsides with loose types of soil need more protection from winds than grassy pasture areas and humus lowlands. Windbreaks also provide homes, cover, and food for animal wildlife. V. V. N.

Windlass The windlass is a wheel and axle which man uses to raise or pull things. It is used to draw water up from wells. The wheel and axle is one of the six simple machines which make work easier. It can raise heavy loads with only a small force.

One spoke of a wheel is attached to a rotating rod (the axle). A chain or a rope from a heavy weight is wrapped around the rod, and the weight can be lifted by turning the handle and winding the rope up on the rod. The lifting force depends on how long the spoke is in relation to the radius of the rod. The longer the spoke, the greater the lifting force.

The Chinese windlass creates much force by the use of axles of two diameters. A ship windlass is a more complicated apparatus. It is hand, steam, or electrically-driven, with chain wheels to move the anchor chain.

The electrically-driven windlass is generally used to operate a tackle-rigged wire rope. It consists of a drum large enough to contain the hoisting cable when the load is in its upper position, together with a suitable gearset interposed between the winding drum and the driving motor. V. V. N.
SEE ALSO: MACHINES, SIMPLE

Windmill A windmill is usually an arrangement of sails or blades attached to arms that stem from a shaft. When the wind blows, the arms turn, revolving the shaft. The shaft, in turn, can drive machines, such as small sawmills, pumps, or electrical generators.

People have made use of the winds to drive windmills for power for many centuries. Windmills are expensive to install, and they are only as certain as the wind itself.

Five basic types of windmills are: (1) multi-bladed turbine wheel, or American-type; (2) Dutch-type; (3) propeller-type high-speed wheel; (4) rotor-type; and (5) vertical-axis wind turbine.

On *American-type* windmills, a tail, or rudder, is used to keep the wheel facing into the wind. It is regulated in high winds by automatic devices, which swing the wheel out of the wind when it gets too strong.

American · Dutch · Rotor

The *Dutch-type,* with its large four-sided wheel, is quite efficient. It is difficult to regulate and operate, however, and has a high first cost. Its speed is regulated by turning the movable top of the tower into the wind.

The *propeller-type* windmill, developed during World War I, was used for aircraft generator drive. The propeller could have two or three blades. The size of the blades is controlled by the size of the generator they are turning. It is a high-speed wheel, enabling the generator to be coupled directly to its shaft. By adjusting the pitch of the blades, its speed can be regulated.

The *rotor* has the ability to start in very low winds. With constant rotor rpm, the wheel is automatically regulated, since an increase in wind speed above the expected condition leaves the rotative force on the rotor unchanged unless the rpm of the rotor also increases. After the designated value of wind velocity is exceeded, the delivery power remains constant. Also, the rotor remains in the most favorable position relative to the direction of the wind.

The *vertical-axis wind turbine* uses long vertical blades attached top and bottom to the windmill shaft. These blades drive the generator.

Energy shortages have led to a new interest in windmills. Unlike fossil fuels, wind is continuously being renewed. Windmills could save tremendous amounts of oil each year. Windmills can be used in conjunction with regular power sources. When the wind does not blow, a customer could draw electricity from a conventional power source. But when the wind blows, the windmills could feed electricity into the commercial power network. Thus the customer would pay for the electricity com- ing into the house, and be paid for the electricity going out of the home. Windmills take energy out of the environment without polluting the environment.   V.V.N./A.J.H.

Windpipe see Respiratory system

Winter see Seasons

Winter sleep see Hibernation

Wire recorder see Sound recording

Wireless see Radio

Wisteria (wiss-TIHR-ee-uh) Wisteria are beautiful vines with twining stems. Each single leaf is made of many leaflets. This flowering plant lives year after year but drops its leaves in late fall. The wisteria is in the pea family.

Clusters of white or purple flowers, which bloom in early summer, are a feature of the American wisteria. The flowers mature into a fruit of beanlike pods. The Chinese wisteria has blue flowers. Its stem may be 100 feet (30 meters) long. The Japanese wisteria has flowers of white, pink, or lavender. The hardy, woody wisteria is a highly prized garden vine.   H.J.C.

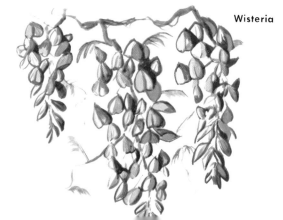

Wisteria

Fall-blooming witch hazel

Courtesy Society For Visual Education, Inc.

North American timber wolf

Witch hazel The witch hazel bush, or tree, acts "bewitched" for it does not bloom in spring as most shrubs do, but in fall when its yellowed leaves are falling. The tiny, yellow clusters of blossoms appear on branches which still hold the ripening seed pods remaining from the last fall's flowers. The seed pods pop open, shooting the seed in the air.

SEE: SHRUB

Wöehler, Friedrich (1800-1882) Friedrich Wöehler was an outstanding German chemist. When he was twenty-seven years old, Wöehler obtained metallic aluminum by heating aluminum chloride with potassium. Then the following year he isolated BERYLLIUM. His greatest contribution to the progress of chemistry, however, was the synthesis of UREA, a crystalline compound containing nitrogen.

Urea is the main solid part of the urine of man and other mammals. Synthesis is the process of making a compound by the union of simpler compounds or of its elements; the formation of urea was important because this was the first time anyone had made an organic compound from inorganic material.

Wöehler was born in Eschersheim, near Frankfurt-am-Main, on July 31, 1800. He was educated at Marburg and Heidelberg universities where he studied to be a physician and surgeon; later he accepted his professor's advice when he suggested that Wöehler give up medicine and devote his life to chemistry.

In 1836 he was invited to become the professor of chemistry at the Göttingen medical school. While he was there, he attracted and trained many young chemists who became prominent throughout the world. D. H. J.

Wolf The wolf is a fierce animal that lives in the forests of the north. It is closely related to the DOG, the fox, and the jackal. Wolves have powerful teeth that can tear and rip the living animals that they hunt. Sometimes they hunt in large groups, called *packs.* In such numbers they can kill and eat very large animals.

In many areas wolves are in danger of extinction. When people cut down a forest, they destroyed the homes of the wolves. Also, people often killed the animals to protect themselves. Most of the wolves today live far north in Canada or in Siberia, sometimes as far north as the tundra regions.

Most wolves are from 3½ to 5 feet (1 to 1.5 meters) long, including their long bushy tails. The color of their hair varies with the species. The small European wolf is reddish-yellow or grayish-yellow. The long shaggy hair of the Tibetan wolf is almost all black. The maned wolf of South America has a reddish coat that becomes black on the legs. The large North American wolf, made famous by writers of early America, is often called the *gray wolf.* It is also known as the *timber wolf.*

Most wolves have nocturnal habits, doing most of their hunting at night. Although they are normally predators when prey is scarce they will become scavengers. Then they eat carrion (dead flesh), fruits, and berries.

The home of wolves, called *dens* or *lairs,* may be a hollow tree, a small cave, a thicket of bushes, or even a hole in the ground. During spring, the female wolf gives birth to three to nine cubs. They are very similar to dogs in the way they spend the first several months of their lives. J.F.B.

Wolfram see Tungsten

Wolverine

Wolverine (wool-ver-EEN) The wolverine is a fierce animal the size of a small dog. It lives in northern Asia, in Europe, and in North America north of the United States. It is a flesh eater of the WEASEL family. In England and Europe it is named *glutton*.

The wolverine is heavily built, and has a pointed face, small ears, and very sharp claws. Discounting wild stories of its cunning and malicious destructiveness, this animal is nevertheless clever and can be extremely destructive, especially if trapped or annoyed. Though not native there, the wolverine is Michigan's state animal. D. J. I.

Womb see Pregnancy

Australian wombat

Wombat (WAHM-batt) Wombats live in Australia. They are small, furry, brown animals with round bodies, short stubby legs, and no tails. They have sharp claws that they use to dig long tunnels where they spend most of their time alone. The female bears one young wombat at a time and carries it in her pouch. Wombats are *marsupials,* mammals with pouches.

Wombats are shy and gentle and make friendly pets; but when frightened or angry, they will bite with their large teeth. They are nocturnal animals, sleeping through the day and searching for food at night.

Wombats are vegetarians. They eat grasses, roots and young tree bark. Their teeth are strong and keep growing all the time. Fossils of larger wombats have been found in Pleistocene deposits in Australia. C. L. K.
SEE ALSO: AUSTRALIA, MAMMALIA, MARSUPIAL

Wood see Forestry, Forest Products, Lumber

Wood duck see Ducks

Wood pulp see Paper

Wood rat see Rodentia

Downy woodpecker

Woodpecker Most woodpeckers are protectors of forests. They eat harmful insects and grubs that live beneath tree bark. The woodpecker finds food by hammering on wood. It drills with its sharp beak, and then "harpoons" insects with its pointed, barbed tongue. Nuts and berries form a small part of its diet.

All woodpeckers nest in holes of trees and poles. All lay white eggs. Short, stiff tails, and four-toed feet support their bodies as they cling to tree trunks. The northern black-backed and boreal woodpeckers are the only types with three toes and without some red coloring. The yellow-bellied sapsucker girdles trunks with borings and thus is one of the few woodpeckers that could prove harmful to trees. J. A. D.

Wool Wool is animal fiber used for spinning yarn. The best-known wool comes from SHEEP. Other wools from such animals as the goat, camel, and vicuna, are straighter and more hairlike.

Wool has a resiliency which makes it one of the finest fibers for cloth. It is naturally kinked because it is composed of overlap-

Shearing sheep to obtain fleece for wool

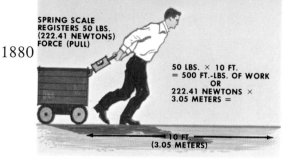

Work = Force X Distance

ping scales. The curliness makes it spring back after stretching. In this way, wrinkles in wool cloth tend to "hang out."

Wool is cut from sheep as *fleece* in one great piece which looks like a sheepskin. In processing, the fleece is pulled apart, cleaned, and sorted according to fineness. Fibers are carded, or straightened, and sorted to length. They are arranged into *rovings, loose ropes;* these ropes are later twisted by spinning to form threads which, in turn, are dyed and woven. 　　　　　　　　　D. J. I.

Wool fat see Lanolin

Work In the science of PHYSICS, work is a basic term used to express the result of a force, such as push or pull, acting in the same direction as the motion it produces. Without either a force or motion, no work is done. Energy is needed to do work.

For example, if a person were to push on a brick wall with 100 pounds (444.8 newtons) of force but the wall did not move, no work would be done regardless of the effort spent. Similarly, the earth orbiting around the sun results in a great amount of motion; however, no force exists in the direction of orbit. Therefore, no work is done.

Work can be expressed in the following formula: Work = Force × Distance. In the English system, FORCE is measured in pounds while distance is measured in feet. Work then has the units of *foot-pounds.* In the metric system, force is measured in dynes and distance in centimeters; the unit of work is the erg. Another unit of work in the metric system is the joule. The joule is defined as the amount of work done by the newton of force (100,000 dynes) acting

over a distance of one meter (100 centimeters).

Note that the time needed to accomplish work has no effect on the value of work. For example, a boy pulling a cart with a force of 50 pounds (222.41 newtons) for 10 feet (3.05 meters) does 50 lbs. × 10 ft. = 500 ft.-lbs. or 678 joules of work. It makes no difference whether it takes 10 seconds or 10 hours, the work done is the same.

Two general rules should be kept in mind when computing the work formula:

(1) The force exerted should be constant over the entire distance. In the previous example, the boy would have to pull with 50 pounds (222.41 newtons) of force over each of the 10 feet (3.05 meters).

(2) The force must act in the same direction as the path of the motion. If the boy were pulling a sled with a rope that was inclined 30° with a force of 10 pounds (44.48 newtons) for a distance of 100 feet (30.48 meters), the work would not equal 1000 ft.-lbs. (1355 joules), for the force was at an angle to the direction of motion. Using trigonometry, the component of the 10-pound force at a 30° angle is computed to be 8.66 pounds (38.52 newtons) in the direction of motion. The answer, therefore, is 8.66 lbs. × 100 ft. = 866 ft.-lbs. (1174 joules).

In order to do work, it is always necessary for a force to overcome resistance. This resistance may take form as FRICTION. For simplicity the examples given consider resistance as zero, otherwise calculations become involved. Once initial resistance is overcome, the force required to move an object is not necessarily the weight of the object, for weight acts only vertically. To pull a 50-pound (22.68-kilogram) sled might require only a 10-pound (44.48-newton) force on level ground. As the slope increases, the force required also increases. When the slope is vertical, the force required will be a lifting force of 50 pounds (222.41 newtons). 　　　　　E.I.D.

SEE ALSO: ENERGY; FOOT-POUND; HORSE-POWER; MACHINES, SIMPLE.

Worm Worms are long, slender, soft-bodied adult animals without jointed appendages (legs). They are *bilaterally symmetrical,* or alike on both sides of the body. Earthworms, flatworms, and tapeworms are examples of true worms. Sometimes beetle larvae and caterpillars are called worms. The *inchworm* or *measuring worm* is the larva of a family of moths. These are not true worms because they are larvae instead of adults, have biting mouth parts and jointed appendages.

In addition to the more common worms, such as earthworms, flatworms, and roundworms, there are about nineteen groups of worms well-known to the scientist but not, as a rule, to the nonscientist. Most of these are marine (live in the sea) or are parasites.

The ribbon worms *(Nemertinea)* are long slender worms flat on the top and bottom. They are often brightly colored with a long extension *(proboscis)* housed in a sheath at the anterior end. The proboscis is shot out the front end, and wraps itself around its prey. A sticky mucus, or a slimy material, often poisonous, entangles, and holds the captured animal, which is usually an annelid, a small fish, or a crustacean.

The horsehair worms *(Nematomorphora)* are long, thread-like worms that, except for one marine species, are found in fresh water. The larvae are parasites in grasshoppers, beetles, and crickets. They develop in the bodies of these insect hosts, and leave as male and female adults. The adults find their way to water where they mate and soon die. Their digestive tracts are not well-developed, and the adults never feed.

Spiny-headed worms *(Acanthocepha)* are parasites in vertebrates, usually fish, pigs, or birds. The worm clings to the host's intestines by means of its spiny head. It ranges in size from 1 inch (2.5 centimeters) to more than 2 feet (61 centimeters), the male being smaller than the female. Eggs develop in the female and are shed as young larvae enclosed in a spiny shell. After passing out with the host's intestinal waste, they live in soil for about three years. When swallowed by insect larvae, they continue to develop. Birds, fish, or pigs eat infected lar-

1—Clamworm, a marine burrowing worm
2—A nemertean ribbon worm
3—Tube worm, a true annelid, builds and lives in a tube
4—A marine nematode, representative of the roundworms

Photos by J. W. Thompson

vae and also become infected.

Arrow worms *(Chaetognatha)* are common in sea water, but are difficult to see because they are transparent. The worms are ¾ to 4 inches (1.9 to 10.2 centimeters) long, and each has a rounded hood on its anterior end. On their sides and tail are thin fins supported by very thin rays. There are no muscles; the fins are used for balance not locomotion.

Underneath the hood is a pair of crescent-shaped hooks set with movable spines. These act as jaws. Between the jaws and around the slit-like mouth are many short bristles. The digestive tract is a simple, straight tube. There are no special respiratory, excretory

✳ **THINGS TO DO**

MAKING A WORMERY

1 gallon = 3.8 liters

1 **Fill a large gallon glass jar or old aquarium with alternate layers of garden soil, a leaf mold, and sand.**

2 **Sprinkle each layer with a little water. On the top of the last layer place small pieces of leafy vegetable and a handful of cornmeal.**

3 **Dig up several earthworms from the yard and transfer them to their new home.**

4 **Cover the sides of the jar for a week to encourage the worms to tunnel near the glass.**

5 **As the earthworms consume the decayed vegetation, they will keep turning the soil.**
   The worms will reproduce and furnish a ready supply of food for pet amphibians and reptiles, or for bait during the fishing season.

or circulatory systems. The nervous system consist of a brain, a few nerves, and some eye spots.

The acorn worms *(Hemichordata)* are found in U- or Y-shaped tunnels in the sand and mud of the seashore. These burrowing worms, about 5 to 6 inches (12.7 to 15.2 centimeters) long, are unsegmented, and have a swollen region upon their anterior ends. The enlarged, swollen region is a collar extending around the anterior end of the worm. Anterior to the collar is a thick proboscis used for burrowing in the sand, while posterior to the collar is a long trunk region.

WRENS

The winter and house wrens are familiar sights

In the posterior part of the proboscis is a stiffening rod, or notochord. Along the side of the pharynx are gill slits. The *notochord* and gill slits have often placed the acorn worms with the *chordates*. At the present time they are put in a separate phylum and are thought of as being halfway between *echinoderms* and chordates. J.C.K.

SEE ALSO: ANIMALS, CLASSIFICATION OF; ANNELIDA; NEMATHELMINTHES; PLATYHELMINTHES

Wound A wound is any break in the surface of the body or other membrane caused either by surgery or by accidental injury. Infection results when germs enter the body through a wound. Healing of a wound depends on new cell growth and the clearing up of any infection.

SEE ALSO: INFECTION, SCAR

Wren Wrens are small birds. Their dull brown coloring matches their surroundings. A few species have a white line over the eye or sometimes black and white stripes on their backs. Wrens have slender bills and short tails cocked up over their backs. They make large nests of grass and twigs in which they lay five to ten eggs.

Wrens belong to a family by themselves. It is one of the few bird families with more species in the New World than the Old World. Only about 30 of the 250 or more named species of wrens are Old World.

Most wrens are active little birds who live in thickets. A few are marsh or rock dwellers. When alarmed, they make harsh chattering sounds, but at other times, they sing tunefully. J. C. K.

Orville and Wilbur Wright with their airplane at Kittyhawk

Wright, Orville and Wilbur (Orville, 1871-1948; Wilbur, 1867-1912) The Wright brothers invented and built the first practical airplane. Gliders had been flown without engines, and balloons had been flown with engines, but their plane was the first powered *heavier-than-air* craft to take off and land safely. They also built its gasoline engine. Orville piloted its first flight at Kitty Hawk, North Carolina, December 17, 1903. It weighed 750 pounds (340 kilograms), had a wing span of 40 feet (12 meters), and cost under $1,000 to build.

Orville and Wilbur Wright lived most of their lives in Dayton, Ohio. Their parents' large library contained many books on science, and the boys read them all. Their first business venture was a weekly newspaper, for which they built the printing press themselves. In 1893, they gave up the newspaper and opened a bicycle shop. Because they made and repaired bicycles, some people assumed they were simply mechanics who invented the airplane by tinkering around. They regarded themselves as scientists, and they could not have done what they did without first studying all that had been written about aeronautics and then conducting their own experiments. They built their own wind tunnel and experimented with model gliders. They also studied the flight of birds. They found by their experiments, that much of what they had read was inaccurate, but it gave them some figures from which to start their own aeronautical calculations.

At Kitty Hawk, which they chose because it had strong air currents, they began building full-scale gliders in 1900. Three years later, when they built their powered plane, they had to design a propeller for it. The available propellers were not right.

In 1904 and 1905 they made more than one hundred and fifty flights, using the second plane they built. News of their flights was published in the *Scientific American* and in European journals, and the British government sent men to investigate. French and German syndicates made offers to buy the Wright invention for their governments. The brothers held off, because they wanted their own government to have the first choice. They could not get anyone from the War Department even to come and watch a demonstration of flight until 1908. Then they gave a series of demonstrations in Virginia for thousands of spectators. The American public was at last convinced that flying was possible, and so was the Government, which paid the Wrights $30,000 for their machine, less than they could have obtained for it abroad.

Even then they did not expect that airplanes would ever be able to go more than 100 miles (161 kilometers) an hour, and they thought the high cost of their fuel would keep planes from being an important form of transportation. Orville lived to see his hopes exceeded, but Wilbur died in 1912, before aviation had fulfilled much of its beginning promise.   M.R.B.

SEE ALSO: AERONAUTICS, AIRCRAFT, AVIATION

Wrought iron see Iron

Xanthophyll (ZANN-thoh-fill) Xanthophyll is the yellow PIGMENT, or coloring matter, in the cells of plants. The yellow in autumn leaves, vegetables, and many flowers is caused by xanthophyll, or xanthophyll combined with other pigments.

The xanthophyll in a plant cell is found in a kind of *plastid,* called a *chromoplast.* PLASTIDS are living bits of *cytoplasm* specialized to store pigments or starch.

In the higher plants, about fifteen to twenty chemical varieties of xanthophyll have been found. *Lutein* is the most important pigment of the group. The yellow color of egg yolk is mostly caused by lutein. In man, xanthophyll absorbed from food is deposited in fat cells and skin tissues.   J. C. K.

Xenon (ZEE-nahn) Xenon is the densest of the group of rare gases in air. It is scarce. Twenty million quarts (19 million liters) of air (the size of several large gymnasiums) would contain only 1 quart (.9 liter) of xenon.

Xenon was discovered by Sir William Ramsay and Morris W. Travis in 1898. Xenon is colorless and odorless. It is called an inert gas, because it does not easily react with other substances.

The characteristics of the inert gases have undergone study. A Canadian chemist synthesized the first compound of xenon, *xenon platinum hexafluoride.* Soon after, Argonne National Laboratory made *xenon tetrafluoride* by a special process. The inert gases are perhaps not as inert as was thought.

Xenon (symbol Xe) has atomic number 54. Its atomic weight is 131.30.   D. A. B.

SEE ALSO: ATOM, ELEMENTS

Xerography (zee-ROG-raf-ee) Xerography is a process by which printed pages, pictures, and maps can be copied quickly. It is a widely used copying process in education, science, and industry.

Xerography is a photographic reproduction of images that uses STATIC ELECTRICITY. In the process, layers of the element SELENIUM are deposited in dry powder form on aluminum or brass plates. The selenium layer, being sensitive to light, provides good *photoconductivity.* An electrical charge across the plates induces a difference of voltage. When the image being duplicated is subjected to a light source such as an electric bulb, the electrostatic-voltage differences cause the contrasting shades or intensities of the image to be transferred to the copy paper, known as the *photoreceptor.* Xerography comes from two Greek words: *xeros* (dry) and *graphos,* (writing).

In 1938 Chester F. Carlson invented the process of reproducing by a proper balance of electrostatic and photographic techniques. With help from the Battelle Memorial Institute, Carlson patented both his electrophotographic method and a workable machine to copy many kind of images. The Xerox Corporation is the only licensee of Carlson's xerographic process. The copies now known as *Xerox* copies are produced and used throughout the world.   H. P. O.

SEE ALSO: PHOTOGRAPHY, PRINTING

X rays In 1895 WILHELM CONRAD ROENTGEN was experimenting with CATHODE rays (electrons) at the University of Würzburg in Germany. While studying the fluorescence caused by cathode rays, he worked in a darkroom and covered the tube with a box to prevent any visible light given off by the tube from escaping. However, Roentgen observed that a screen coated with barium platinocyanide glowed brilliantly when brought near the covered tube.

In a scientific report, Roentgen listed almost all the important properties of X rays. He noted that the rays could penetrate ½

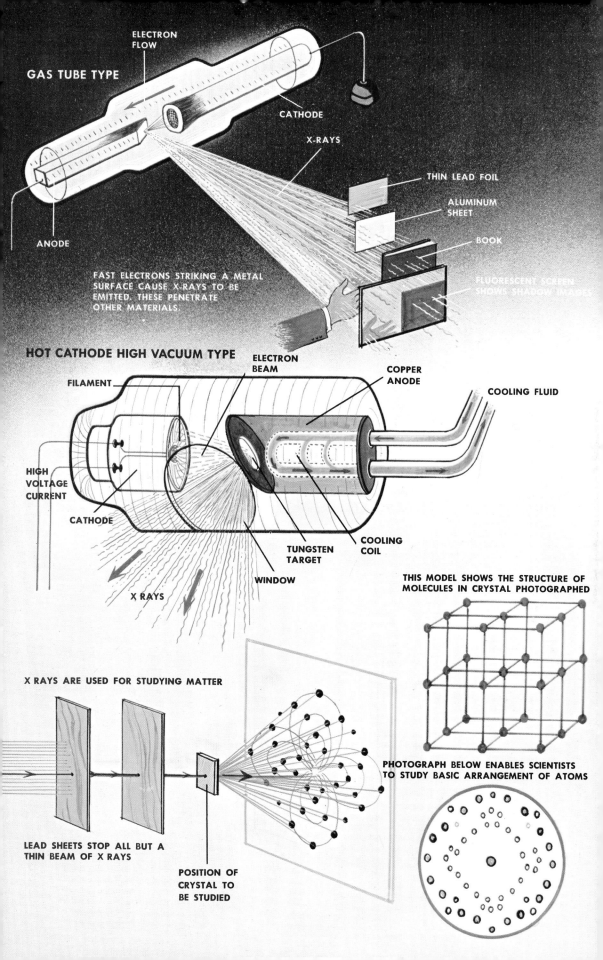

GAS TUBE TYPE

ELECTRON FLOW

CATHODE

X-RAYS

THIN LEAD FOIL

ALUMINUM SHEET

BOOK

FLUORESCENT SCREEN SHOWS SHADOW IMAGES

ANODE

FAST ELECTRONS STRIKING A METAL SURFACE CAUSE X-RAYS TO BE EMITTED. THESE PENETRATE OTHER MATERIALS.

HOT CATHODE HIGH VACUUM TYPE

ELECTRON BEAM

FILAMENT

COPPER ANODE

COOLING FLUID

HIGH VOLTAGE CURRENT

CATHODE

TUNGSTEN TARGET

COOLING COIL

WINDOW

X RAYS

THIS MODEL SHOWS THE STRUCTURE OF MOLECULES IN CRYSTAL PHOTOGRAPHED

X RAYS ARE USED FOR STUDYING MATTER

LEAD SHEETS STOP ALL BUT A THIN BEAM OF X RAYS

POSITION OF CRYSTAL TO BE STUDIED

PHOTOGRAPH BELOW ENABLES SCIENTISTS TO STUDY BASIC ARRANGEMENT OF ATOMS

inch (1.3 centimeters) of wood and that, when he placed his hand between the cathode-ray and the fluorescent screen, the shadows of his bones were visible. He reported that X rays affected photographic film, too.

To understand how X rays are produced, imagine a machine gun firing bullets in rapid succession against a steel block. Anyone standing near the block can hear sound-wave pulses as the bullets strike it. The generating of X rays is similar. The electrons act like bullets and produce X-ray waves as they hit a target.

Roentgen reasoned that these X rays were a new form of ELECTROMAGNETIC *radiation* spreading out from the spot hit by the electrons. However, these rays acted more like waves than like electron particles. Historically, this marked science's first experience with matter showing the now-famous *particle-and wave* nature. Light and other radiation is now known to show this same *dual* nature.

X rays traveling in empty space are electromagnetic in nature. They are the same type of radiation as ordinary light, infrared light, ultraviolet light, and radio waves. The electromagnetic tradition of the X-ray range has a wavelength of about 10^8 cm and a corresponding frequency of about 3×10^{18} vibrations per second. The emission or absorption of X rays, however, takes place only with unit amount of the energy carried by the X rays being absorbed or emitted. That is, in their interaction with matter, X rays have the properties of particles rather than waves. Such X-ray packets are called X-ray photons and the energy carried by one photon is called a quantum.

X rays are ordinarily generated by a highly evacuated tube called a Coolidge tube after its inventor, W. D. Coolidge. The cathode is a fine tungsten wire (filament) placed at the center of a hollow cup. The cup focuses the filament's electron stream toward the target plate. The filament is electrically heated to the desired temperature. The anode (target) is a hollow tungsten or molybdenum rod, cooled internally by running water. The X rays emerge around the target.

No current or rays come from an X-ray tube until the cathode is red-hot and gives off electrons. The degree of penetration or "hardness" of the X rays is related to the speed of the electrons striking the target. This speed is proportional to the voltage across the tube.

X-ray tubes intended for examining biological tissues require at least 35,000 volts. Bone thicknesses (and fractures) are best seen with 45,000 volts. X rays need to be used with care to avoid harmful effects. X rays serve numerous uses in medicine, industry, and research.　　　D. A. B.

SEE ALSO: ELECTRONICS, FLUOROSCOPE

XY chromosomes see Heredity

Xylem (ZYE-lemm) Inside a plant are groups of cells which do a particular job for the plant. Xylem cells are conducting tubes which carry the raw materials from the roots up to the leaves for use in the manufacture of food. A layer of xylem cells is made during every growing season of a plant's life. These layers form the ANNUAL RINGS. All the cells in the wood of a tree are xylem cells. Heartwood, sapwood, knots, and the grain of lumber all occur in xylem tissue.

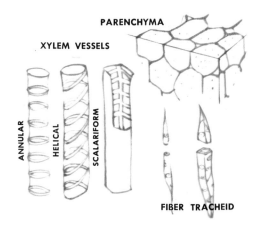

Five types of xylem cells

Xylem cells are usually found toward the center of roots, stems, and leaves. They form a continuous column of vascular tissue. There are four kinds of cells in xylem. *Parenchyma* is a large, thin-walled storage cell. *Fibers* have thickened walls and give support and strength to the plant. *Tracheids* are elongated single cells for strength and conduction. A *vessel* is a series of cells stacked one on the other. The constant pull of liquids upward has destroyed the cross wall and made a long tube.　　　H.J.C.

Yam vine and root

Yam Yam is the root of a vine. In tropical countries, it is eaten in place of the potato. It is not a SWEET POTATO, for it belongs to another family. Yams are larger, sweeter, and oranger than sweet potatoes.

This climbing vine has clusters of small green flowers, winged seeds, and heart-shaped flowers and leaves. It is a native of South Sea islands and India. One variety grows to 8 feet (2.4 meters), and weighs 100 pounds (45 kilograms).

One variety is raised for medicinal purposes. CORTISONE is extracted from it. Louisiana leads in its production.   P.G.B.

Yawn Yawning is an involuntary, wide opening of the mouth with inhalation and exhalation of breath. It is usually caused by being tired, bored, or even hungry. Human beings and many animals yawn.

Yawning occurs when large quantities of air are slowly inhaled and then gradually exhaled. If yawning occurs too often, it may be symptomatic of disease. It may mean that the body is not getting enough oxygen.

M. R. L.

Yaws Yaws is a common tropical disease found in the Caribbean, the Philippine Islands, Africa, the East Indies, and other tropical regions. It is caused by bacteria-like micro-organisms called *spirochetes* which attack primarily children.

Symptoms are dull pains in the joints, loss of weight, and a loss of appetite. Yellowish sores appear, gradually forming larger raspberry-shaped swellings which give off a contagious substance. If the organisms in this substance come into contact with an open wound directly or through carriers such as flies, infection occurs. Yaws may be cured by injections of penicillin.   M. R. L.
SEE ALSO: SPIROCHETES

Year see Calendar, Earth

Yak

Yak (YACK) The yak is a central Asian ox. It belongs in the ungulate group along with CATTLE and BUFFALO. Yaks are common on the high snowy plateaus, or flatlands, in the mountains of Tibet. It is the largest animal native to that country. The animal lives best in high altitudes, and can endure very low temperatures. Extreme heat is fatal to the yak.

The wild yaks are very shy, but if angered they can be dangerous. They crush their victims by falling upon them. They feed upon mountain plants, and even in captivity will not eat grain.

A yak has a massive, compact body with short neck and legs. The head appears small compared to the bulk of its body. Some yaks are hornless, but most have heavy, rather thick horns. A fringe of long, silky hair grows down from the shoulders, along the sides, and over the thighs. The tail is also covered with long flowing hair.

These animals have been domesticated and also bred with cattle. The hybrid is called a *hainyak*. Yaks are used as beasts of burden, and are valued for their milk, meat, and hair. The milk is rich and makes good butter. The long, silky hair is woven into cloth and made into rope.   J. C. K.
SEE ALSO: ARTIODACTYLA, OXEN

✳ THINGS TO DO

WHAT MAKES BREAD DOUGH RISE?

1   **Puncture an opening in a metal cover of a glass jar. Insert one end of a length of a rubber hose or glass tube through the hole. Place melted wax around the hole to insure an airtight connection. Submerge the other end of the tube in a glass of lime water.**

2   **Combine one cup of flour, one tablespoon of sugar, one-fourth package of commercial yeast, and one-half cup of water. Place this mixture into the glass jar. Screw on the top immediately.**

3   **Set this equipment in a warm place. Soon the dough will rise. Remove the lid, puncture the mound of dough, and quickly seal it again. The gas that caused the bread to rise escapes into the tube that leads to the limewater. If this gas is carbon dioxide, the limewater will turn milky.**

Yeast   Yeast is a microscopic plant that can ferment sugars and starches to make alcohol and carbon dioxide gas. Thus yeast is used in baking because the gas formed causes dough to expand; and it is grown with many kinds of plant juices to make ethyl alcohol for beverages and other uses.

Individual yeast plants are oval, single cells. Wild yeasts rest in the soil during the winter, and in spring are carried about by wind and insects. In this resting stage, yeasts can stand dryness and cold, but are killed by heat near 212° F. (100° C.).

Dried yeast cells were found to exist as early as 2000 B.C., but scientific knowledge of yeasts came with the cell theory.

Yeast-cell plants reproduce by a process called *budding.* New cell-buds may be formed every 20 to 30 minutes by yeast growing in sugary or starchy foods that are warm (80° to 90° F. or 27° to 32° C.) and moist. Each yeast cell secretes several enzymes, one of which can break down starches into simpler sugars. Another yeast enzyme can change sugar into alcohol, carbon dioxide, and free energy. The yeast cells use the energy and some of the sugar for growth processes.

The chemical equation for this yeast activity on glucose sugar is:

$$C_6H_{12}O_6 \text{(glucose)} \rightarrow C_2H_5OH + 2CO_2 + \text{energy}$$

In making bread, the CO_2 gas forms bubbles that lighten *(leaven)* the dough.

The same species of yeast plant may come in subspecies used for different purposes

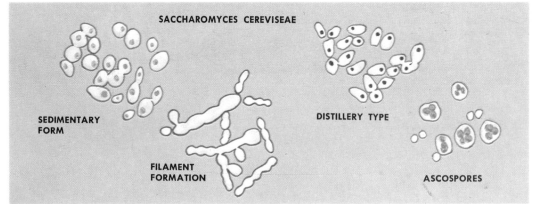

SACCHAROMYCES CEREVISEAE

SEDIMENTARY FORM

FILAMENT FORMATION

DISTILLERY TYPE

ASCOSPORES

Before yeast was commercially grown, each household kept either a pot of potato water or a pan of sour dough as a ferment starter. These were wild yeast gardens, to be drawn upon for the family baking or brewing. Modern commercial yeast production includes the careful cultivation of special strains of the yeast species, *Saccharomyces cereviseae*. Bakers' yeasts are strains that stop fermentation when enough CO_2 gas and only 4 to 5 per cent alcohol are formed, while brewers' yeast strains grow in plant juices until 14 to 17% alcohol is made.

Yeast is biologically a fungus of the class *Ascomycetes*. Besides multiplying asexually by budding, yeasts also have sexual reproduction in which two cells unite to form a fertilized cell, or *zygote*. The zygote divides to form a four-celled spore case, or *ascus*. When the ascus breaks, the four spores scatter in the air. When they alight where there is food, they grow as new yeast plants.

E. M. S.

SEE ALSO: FERMENTATION, FUNGUS, SPORE FORMATION

Yellow fever Yellow fever is caused by a VIRUS and at one time was common in Africa and South America. Human beings get the disease from the bite of infected mosquitoes. In severe cases the liver is involved, and the skin becomes yellow because of JAUNDICE.

Along with jaundice and high fever, symptoms include headache, backache, and internal bleeding or hemorrhage. In early stages of the disease, the edges and tip of the tongue are bright red, but later become brownish. In severe cases the death rate is high.

Fever is the only common symptom in a mild case, and fortunately most cases are mild. After recovery people are immune for the rest of their lives.

Before it was known that yellow fever is transmitted by mosquitos, hundreds of people died from it each year. Today, mosquito control and the development of a vaccine have almost eliminated the disease from the modern world.   J.C.K.

SEE ALSO: MOSQUITO; REED, WALTER

Yellow jacket see Wasp

Yellow River see Asia

Yew tree and leaves

Yew The yew is an evergreen tree or bush. It has dark, shiny, green, flat leaves that grow in a row down each side of the stem. The "fruit" is like a small red "berry."

Because of its dense growth, the yew makes an excellent hedge, and in formal gardens is often clipped into interesting shapes. The foliage is poisonous, however, and animals have been poisoned by eating it.

Beautifully grained yew wood is used in cabinetmaking and in canoe paddles; because of its strength and elasticity, it makes the best archery bows.

There are many varieties of yew, ranging from the ground-hugging Americans yew to the Pacific yew, a 50-foot (15-meter) tree.

J.M.C.

Yolk Yolk is found in egg cells. It is food for the developing young animal. Yolk of the mammal egg is very small. Yolk of the frog egg is larger. The yolk of the bird egg is the largest. The embryo bird develops around the yolk and leaves the shell with a supply of

Four main substances in yolk

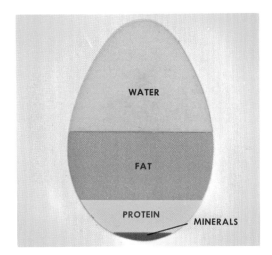

WATER

FAT

PROTEIN

MINERALS

food (yolk) in the bird's crop.

The location of yolk in the *cytoplasm* varies. Mammalian eggs, in which the yolk is small though evenly distributed, are called *isolecithal* eggs. They divide into cells of equal size as the young animal forms. Frog eggs have more yolk. It is concentrated on one side (*vegetal pole*). The nucleus and most of the cytoplasm is found on the opposite side (*animal pole*). In this type *(telolecithal),* division is unequal; the yolk-laden cells divide more slowly. In bird eggs, with large amounts of yolk, cell division occurs only at the animal pole, with the embryo developing on top of the yolk.

J. C. K.

SEE ALSO: EMBRYOLOGY, VITAMINS

Ytterbium (ih-TER-bee-uhn) Ytterbium is the 70th element and in the lanthanide series of rare earth elements. It was isolated in 1907, and is found in a number of different minerals.

Ytterbium can be separated from minerals such as gadolinite and xenotine, and it has been purified. Some of its known salts are the oxide, hydroxide, chloride, nitrate, and sulfate. The chloride, nitrate, and sulfate salts have at least one molecule of water present in each molecule of salt. There are a great many isotopes of ytterbium. Its average atomic weight is 173.04. The chemical symbol is Yb.

M. S.

SEE ALSO: ELEMENTS

Yttrium (IT-tree-um) Yttrium is an element of the rare earth metals. It is a colorless element and is relatively soluble in water. It is one of the most abundant members of the sub-group in which it is sometimes classified.

Yttrium is usually found in combination with gadolinite, xenotine, euxite and fergusonite. It is sometimes classified with the cerium sub-group of rare earths because of the abundance of gadolinium. The element, yttrium, was first discovered with gadolinium in 1794, and later was isolated in comparative purity by Carl G. Mosander in 1873.

Yttrium (chemical symbol Y) is element number 34. Its atomic weight is 88.905.

J. R. S.

SEE ALSO: ATOM, ELEMENTS

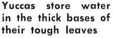

Yuccas store water in the thick bases of their tough leaves

Courtesy Society For Visual Education, Inc.

Courtesy Society For Visual Education, Inc.

The yucca flower protects its nectar from evaporation

Yucca (YUHK-uh) Yucca is the name of many kinds of plants found in southwestern United States, Mexico, and Central America. They vary in size from shrubs to trees over 30 feet (9 meters) tall. Stems may be fibrous or woody. Yuccas are evergreens, retaining their leaves from year to year. Well-known yuccas are the giant JOSHUA TREE and Adam's Needle.

The leaves of the yucca are grouped at branch ends. They are narrow and pointed and usually stiff with rough edges. The plants produce white or greenish-white bell-shaped flowers. They hang downward in clusters from a stem surrounded by leaves. The ovary produced is in three parts. In some it may form into a juicy berry fruit or in others develop into dry pods.

Yucca plants have a peculiar process of reproduction. Fertilization by cross pollination can be accomplished only by the yucca moths, of which there are different species for each kind of yucca. The larvae of the moth feed on yucca seeds. The female lays four or five eggs in the pistil of a flower then plugs it up with a ball of pollen from another flower. Thus the plant is fertilized. Each larva when hatched eats about twenty seeds, but a flower produces about two hundred, and so there are always enough seeds to form new plants.

D.J.I.

SEE ALSO: DESERT

The zenith and nadir are points above and below a person on Earth

Zenith The zenith is the point directly overhead where an imaginary line from the center of the earth through the observer would intersect the heavens. It is used in astronomical observations. The *nadir* is directly opposite.

Zeppelin see Airship, Dirigible

Zero Zero, represented by the symbol 0, may have several meanings depending on the way it is used. If one boy catches 4 fish and a second catches 0 fish, the 0 indicates the absence of quantity. In the numeral 706, the 0 indicates no tens. On a graduated scale, such as a thermometer, zero identifies the point from which positive or negative temperatures are recorded.

When zero is used on a number line representing the integers, it serves as the separation point for the points which correspond to the positive and negative integers.

$$-4 \quad -3 \quad -2 \quad -1 \quad 0 \quad 1 \quad 2 \quad 3 \quad 4$$

The number 0 has the following properties: If 0 is added to (or subtracted from) any number, the result is the given number. If any number is subtracted from itself, the difference is zero. If any number is multiplied by 0, the product is zero. Zero divided by a non-zero number is zero. A non-zero

Zebra (ZEE-bruh) The only striped member of the HORSE family is the zebra. It is a hoofed mammal with an odd number of toes. Its head and ears are rather large for the rest of its body. The mane is short and stands upright. Zebras are fast runners and band together in herds. They live in the eastern and southern plains of Africa. Grass is their main food.

Zebras are usually wild, though the natives have some success taming them for work and riding. They are becoming scarce since the hide is valued by natives for leather and the meat for food. Hunters are also decreasing the numbers of this beautiful beast. The most dangerous natural enemy is the lion. The zebra's striped body is a natural camouflage. Sharp teeth and great kicking ability also help them survive.

There are several species of zebra. The *grevy* is the largest, from 4½ to 5 feet (1.4 to 1.5 meters) at the shoulder. *Grant's zebra* measures 4½ feet (1.4 meters), *Burchell's* 4 feet, 2 inches (1.3 meters), and the *mountain zebra* only four feet (1.2 meters), the smallest. The last *quagga* (a wild zebra-like animal with reddish stripes) died in 1872. Zebras range in weight from 400 to 700 pounds (180 to 315 kilograms).   H.J.C.

Some uses of the concept zero

EMPTY WIRE OF ABACUS REPRESENTS ZERO

ZERO IS THE BEGINNING POINT IN A GRAPH

number divided by zero would yield a meaningless or undefined quotient. Zero divided by zero would not yield a unique quotient. Therefore zero cannot serve as a divisor. $2 + 0 = 2; 3 - 0 = 3; \frac{0}{4} = 0;$

$8 - 8 = 0; \frac{5}{0}$ undefined; $\frac{0}{0}$ indeterminate.

The term zero also has some special uses. ABSOLUTE ZERO is the temperature a body would have if it had no heat whatsoever (-273.18° C. or -459.69° F.). Arbitrary 0 is zero selected as a convenient reference point, as on a graph or scale.   I.K.F.

SEE ALSO: ALGEBRA, ARITHMETIC, NUMBER SYSTEMS

Zinc   Zinc is a blue-white metallic element. In ancient times, men made objects of brass or bronze, not knowing that zinc was a main ingredient. Today zinc is used in making batteries and galvanized metals. Its chief ores are *blende, calamine, franklinite,* and *Willemite.*

The free element zinc is obtained by roasting one of its ores to zinc oxide and then reducing this oxide with carbon. Finally, the metal is purified by distilling it to resolidify it from the vapor. Besides copper-zinc alloys, zinc forms many other useful alloys used for making springs, type metal, and other products. Its white oxide and related salts are used in paints, plastics, and textiles. Zinc sulfide forms a luminous *phosphor* which coats television tubes and fluorescent lights.

Zinc (symbol Zn) has atomic No. 30. It has an atomic weight of 65.37. Its valence is +2, density 7.14 gm/cc, and melting point over 419° C. (786° F.).   D.A.B.

SEE ALSO: ALLOY, ATOM, ELEMENT

Zinjanthropus   see Evolution of man

Zinnia (ZINN-ee-uh)   Zinnias are brightly-colored flowers that came from Mexico and the southwest part of the United States. They are called COMPOSITE FLOWERS because the parts that look like colored petals are small flowers. The small flowers are grouped to make a flowerhead.

Helen J. Challand
Garden zinnias

The stem is stiff and hairy, and the leaves are rough and somewhat sticky. The flowers range in color from scarlet, salmon, rose, purple, orange, and yellow, to white. Moths and butterflies pollinate zinnias. Zinnias also attract hummingbirds.

The California giant zinnias grow to 3 feet (.9 meter). Flowers of the giant zinnias often exceed 6 inches (15.2 centimeters) across. Zinnias grow well in ordinary well-drained soil with full sun. They grow easily from seeds that germinate in five days. The seeds can be started in a cold frame and transplanted later to open ground.

Dwarf zinnias make attractive border plants. If the flower heads are removed before seeds are formed, the plant will continue to bloom. The double zinnia is of French origin.   P. G. B.

The cut white zircon looks likes a diamond

Zircon (ZER-kahn)   A zircon is a mineral that is found in nearly all igneous and in some metamorphic rocks. Zircons are sometimes found in sandy stream beds and on beaches, but more often in the same waters where prospectors pan for gold.

Most zircons are found in the Ural Mountains of Russia, in Ceylon, in Australia, and in the United States in Florida, California, and Oregon. Some zircons are used in jewelry. These shiny, glittery stones are brittle and chip easily. Colorless zircons that resemble diamonds are called *jargoons.* Transparent stones with a reddish color are called *hyacinth* zircons. Industry uses zircons in making heat-resistant porcelains, chemicals, abrasives, foundry sand, alloys, and in refining zirconium.   M. R. L.

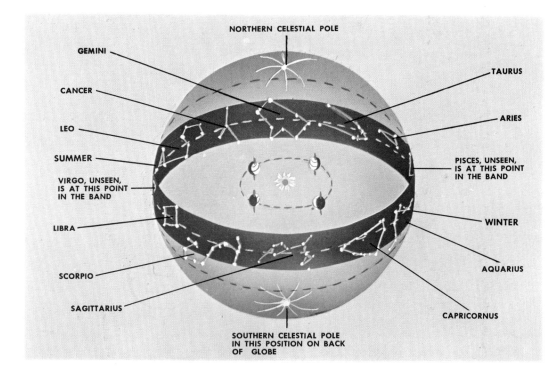

NORTHERN CELESTIAL POLE

GEMINI

TAURUS

CANCER

ARIES

LEO

SUMMER

PISCES, UNSEEN,
IS AT THIS POINT
IN THE BAND

VIRGO, UNSEEN,
IS AT THIS POINT
IN THE BAND

LIBRA

WINTER

SCORPIO

AQUARIUS

SAGITTARIUS

CAPRICORNUS

SOUTHERN CELESTIAL POLE
IN THIS POSITION ON BACK
OF GLOBE

Zirconium (zer-KOH-nee-um) Zirconium is the 40th element. It was discovered in 1789. In its pure state it occurs as a black powder or a gray shiny metal. It is soluble in hydrofluoric acid and aqua regia (nitric and hydrochloric acids). The powder form can be explosive when mixed with oxidizing agents.

Zirconium is very resistant to corrosion and heat, and is therefore important in building atomic reactors. Because of its unstable nature, this element is used in flashbulbs, lamp filaments, and explosive mixtures. Zirconium chloride and hydroxide are used in dyes, the silicate in ceramics, and the oxychloride in antiperspirants.

Zirconium (symbol Zr) has an atomic weight of 91.22. M. S.

SEE ALSO: ATOM, ELEMENTS

Zodiac The earth, the sun, the moon, and most of the planets are almost on the same level. One might say that they are spinning around on a very large saucer in SPACE. The sun is in the middle of the saucer. Far out beyond the path of the farthest planet are stars on this same level. Ancient people recognized twelve constellations that form a background for the imaginary path that the moon, the sun, and the planets trace out in the sky. Eleven of these constellations are animals (including men and women). The twelfth is *Libra, the Scales.* Ancient star watchers gave this band of constellations the name *zodiac.* Zodiac means "of living things."

The zodiac, then, is a circle of twelve constellations that surround man's solar system. The sun, the moon, and most of the planets seem to move along this path in front of these twelve constellations. When the sun is between the earth and a certain constellation of the zodiac, the sun is said to be "in" that constellation. The zodiac is divided into twelve equal parts. The sun occupies each part for about one month. The constellations and the signs of the zodiac are *Leo, Virgo, Libra, Scorpius, Sagittarius, Capricornus, Aquarius, Pisces, Aries, Taurus, Gemini,* and *Cancer.* C. L. K.

SEE ALSO: CONSTELLATION, SOLAR SYSTEM

1. CHAPMAN'S ZEBRA
2. GORILLA (ADULT MALE)
3. INDIAN ELEPHANT
4. FENNEC, A SMALL FOX OF THE SAHARA DESERT
5. BARBARY APE

Courtesy Society For Visual Education, Inc.

Zoo A zoo is a place in which live animals are kept on exhibit for the education of the public and for scientific study. Zoos are usually in parks; the name "zoo" comes from the term *zoological garden.*

Many people who will never be able to travel over the world are able, through the zoo, to see and to learn about the animal life in other countries. Many discoveries about the habits, breeding, and illnesses of animals have been made in zoos. One of the most important contributions of the zoo is that of preserving wildlife which is becoming extinct.

A good zoo creates excellent conditions for the animals. It will have a kitchen for preparing healthful meals that the animals will enjoy. Some zoos even bake a special kind of bread for the bears.

All zoos have some sort of animal hospital. The hospital is usually set apart from the rest of the zoo. In large zoos these hospitals are equipped with X-ray rooms, operating rooms, and quarantine wards just as are hospitals for people. In small zoos, the owner or keeper will often take the sick animal into his own home to try to bring it back to health.

Today, more zoos are trying to place animals in natural settings instead of cages. Natural settings are better for the animals. Scientists can also better study the animals' character and behavior. Modern zoos also have breeding programs. They breed their adult animals in order to continue the species.

Animals for zoos are obtained in various ways. They may be bought from dealers who hire people in foreign countries to capture wild animals, or the zoos themselves may send out hunting expeditions.

Many animals are donated to the zoo. The U.S. Air Force presented the Washington Zoo with the monkey that made the first space trip in a rocket. Of course, many animals are born in a zoo. These may be kept to grow up, or they may be traded to another zoo for an animal the zoo does not have.

Zoos have been in existence for thousands of years because people have always been fascinated by strange animals and by animal life. Kings and wealthy lords were once the owners of the zoos, but today most zoos are owned by cities or zoological societies. J.M.C.

SEE ALSO: ZOOLOGY

A major part of zoology is classification. It may involve working with fossils

Zoology (zoe-AHL-eh-gee) Zoology is the scientific study of animals. Zoologists are interested in the ways animals are alike and unlike. They sort out, or classify, animals, on the basis of their likenesses and differences.

Animals of today are compared with animals that lived millions of years ago. Remains of these very early animals are called *fossils,* and they are found buried beneath the surface of the earth. How the differences between the fossil animals and the present-day animals came about is of interest to zoologists.

Animals are studied by physiologists to find out how they function. Physiologists study such things as how food is digested, how blood cells carry oxygen, how glands work, and how the nervous system carries impulses. The changes that take place in a fertilized egg in order to form a new animal are studied by *embryologists.*

MORPHOLOGY

Morphology includes all the subdivisions, or fields of study, in zoology that have to do with form and structure (parts or systems in an animal body.) In *anatomy,* organ systems such as the digestive system, the muscular system, or the nervous system are observed and described. If the organ systems of different animals are compared, the field of study is known as *comparative* anatomy.

In *histology,* scientists called *histologists* study the tissues that make up organs, comparing and classifying them. In the field of *cytology,* cytologists are interested in the structure of the cells which form the tissues.

Embryologists study the development of a new animal from a fertilized egg.

Paleontologists study the structure of fossils, and try to reconstruct the whole animal from the usually incomplete remains dug up from the earth. By studying the geology of the place where the animal remains were discovered, they try to determine the age of the fossil and the kind of environment in which it probably lived. With this information, plus a reconstruction or likeness of the animal, its relationship to present-day animals can be partially determined.

PHYSIOLOGY

In general, physiologists are interested in how whole animals—all their various organs—function. Physiological chemistry is a study of the chemical processes which occur in living cells, tissues, and organs of an animal body. *Psychology* deals with the way animals behave when acted upon by different influences in their environment.

SYSTEMATIC ZOOLOGY

"Systematic" means "orderly arrangement." Systematic zoology includes all the fields of zoology which make some kind of orderly arrangement. In *taxonomy,* animals are grouped or classified into an orderly arrangement starting with the simpler animals and proceeding to the more complex.

Taxonomists, who classify animal life, draw upon knowledge from other fields of zoology. Classification may be based upon likenesses and differences between animals that were originally described by anatomists. Paleontologists furnish information about earlier types of animals which aids the taxonomist in classifying modern animals.

Ecologists are zoologists who study the relationship between an animal and its environment. They often arrange animals according to their living habits, such as the kinds of foods they eat, whether they are active by day or by night, or whether they hibernate in the winter or migrate to warmer climates. They may also classify animals according to the environments in which they live: deserts, swamps, open seas, forests.

A *zoogeographer* observes, describes, and arranges animals according to their distribution in various parts of the world. He compares the animals in one region with related animals in another place.

EXPERIMENTAL ZOOLOGY

In experimental zoology, the normal animal is changed in some way. There are many ways in which an animal may be changed during the course of an experiment. Any changes in the functioning or behavior of such animals are observed, and the experimental animal is then compared to normal animals and conclusions drawn from the observations. Almost any of the fields of zoology may become experimental.

SPECIALIZED FIELDS

Since there are so many animals in the world and so many ways of studying them, a number of zoologists have become specialists, working with only a single group of animals. To name only a few of these fields, the study of birds is called *ornithology;* the study of parasites, *parasitology;* the study of fish, *ichthyology;* the study of reptiles, *herpetology.*

Each one of these specialized fields may be subdivided in the same manner as the whole field of zoology. For instance, an ornithologist may be interested in zoogeography and describe the distribution of birds. He may be interested in the classification of birds and become a taxonomist for the group. On the other hand, if research is done on migratory, eating, or nesting habits of birds, the emphasis is ecological.

DISADVANTAGES OF RIGID
CLASSIFICATION

Classification of zoology into either large or small subdivisions should not be too rigid or set because there is too much overlapping among the fields of study.

Genetics is a field that is difficult to classify because it can be included under almost any subdivision of zoology. The purpose of genetics is to find out how animal characteristics are transmitted from parent animals to their young. Sometimes genetic research is morphological in that animals with characteristics that have arisen by mutation are described and compared to their parents. Genetics is cytological if the behavior of *chromosomes* (bearing certain genes) is studied. Geneticists interested in how genes work are physiological geneticists. Some groups of geneticists are concerned with mapping locations of genes and arranging them in order upon a chromosome. Because the location of genes is often determined by using X-rays to change normal chromosomes, these studies are examples of experimental and cytological zoology.

Embryology is another field which may be called morphological, systematic, physiological, or experimental, depending upon the type of embryological investigations being made. J. C. K.

SEE ALSO: ANATOMY, BIOCHEMISTRY, ECOLOGY. EMBRYOLOGY, HEREDITY, PALEONTOLOGY, PHYSIOLOGY

Zoophyte (ZOE-uh-fite) Zoophyte is any plantlike animal, such as the coral or the sponge. It has a branched, simple structure. At one time it was classified between plant and animal.

Zygote (ZYE-goht) The zygote is a fertilized egg cell. The male and female sex cells that fuse to form a zygote are called *gametes,* or germ cells. In simple plants or animals, the GAMETES are quite similar. In higher organisms they are of two types—the sperm, or male gamete, and the egg, or female gamete.

Each gamete that makes up the zygote contains half the number of chromosomes (*haploid* number) contained in ordinary body cells. When the gametes fuse to form the zygote, the full number of chromosomes (*diploid* number) is present.

In embryonic development, the zygote goes through cell division called *mitosis,* and in this process a many-celled embryo develops. These cells eventually become specialized into the kinds of cells that make up organ systems such as nerve cells, muscle cells, bones or cartilage cells, and so forth.
E. Y. K.

SEE ALSO: CHROMOSOME, EMBRYOLOGY, FERTILIZATION, HEREDITY, MITOSIS AND MEIOSIS

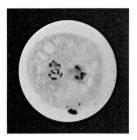

In the zygote, fertilized egg, of the ascaris worm, the chromatin material can be seen
Photo-micrograph by
National Teaching Aids, Inc.

**ANATOMISTS ARE CONCERNED
WITH WHOLE SYSTEM
OF MUSCLES**

PARASITOLOGISTS research
the effect of parasites
upon muscle tissue

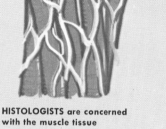

HISTOLOGISTS are concerned
with the muscle tissue

CYTOLOGISTS
are concerned
with muscle cells

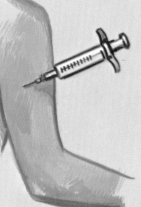

PATHOLOGISTS are concerned
with muscle diseases and
symptoms relating to muscles

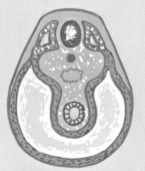

EMBRYOLOGISTS study the development of the muscle in
the embryo

PHYSIOLOGISTS are concerned
with muscular action

Conversion Factors to Metric Measurement

Length
1 inch = 25.4 millimeters (mm) exactly
1 inch = 2.54 centimeters (cm) exactly
1 foot = 0.3048 meters (m) exactly
1 yard = 0.9144 meters (m) exactly
1 mile = 1.609344 kilometers (km) exactly

Area
1 square inch = 6.4516 square centimeters (cm^2) exactly
1 square foot = 0.092903 square meters (m^2)
1 square yard = 0.836127 square meters (m^2)
1 square acre = 0.404686 hectares (ha)
1 square mile = 2.58999 square kilometers (km^2)

Cubic Measure
1 cubic inch = 16.387064 cubic centimeters (cm^3) exactly
1 cubic foot = 0.0283168 cubic meters (m^3)
1 cubic yard = 0.764555 cubic meters (m^3)

US Liquid Measure
1 fluid ounce = 29.5735 milliliters (ml)
1 fluid ounce = 0.2957 deciliters (dl)
1 pint = 0.473176 liters (l)
1 gallon = 3.78541 liters (l)

US Dry Measure
1 pint = 0.550610 liters (l)
1 bushel = 35.2391 liters (l)

Weight
1 grain = 0.0647989 grams (g)
1 ounce = 28.3495 grams (g)
1 pound = 0.453592 kilograms (kg)
1 short ton = 0.907185 metric tons (t)
1 UK ton = 1.01605 metric tons (t)

Temperature
To convert Fahrenheit to Centigrade (Celsius) complete the following equation. $(F° − 32) \times 5 \div 9 = C°$